Leading
with
Soul

Lee G. Bolman

Terrence E. Deal

Leading
with
Soul

An Uncommon Journey of Spirit

Revised Third Edition

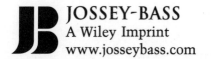

JOSSEY-BASS
A Wiley Imprint
www.josseybass.com

Copyright © 2011 by John Wiley & Sons, Inc. All rights reserved.

Published by Jossey-Bass
A Wiley Imprint
989 Market Street, San Francisco, CA 94103-1741—www.josseybass.com

Interior design by Nancy Sayre Simerly
Illustrations by Barbara Rhodes

Credits are on page 293.

Jossey-Bass books and products are available through most bookstores. To contact Jossey-Bass directly call our Customer Care Department within the U.S. at 800-956-7739, outside the U.S. at 317-572-3986, or fax 317-572-4002.

Jossey-Bass also publishes its books in a variety of electronic formats. Some content that appears in print may not be available in electronic books.

Library of Congress Cataloging-in-Publication Data

Bolman, Lee G.
  Leading with soul : an uncommon journey of spirit / Lee G. Bolman,
Terrence E. Deal. —Rev. 3rd ed.
    p. cm.
  Includes bibliographical references.
  ISBN 978-0-470-61900-1 (hardback); ISBN 978-1-118-06734-5 (ebk);
ISBN 978-1-118-06736-9 (ebk); ISBN 978-1-118-06753-6 (ebk)
  1. Leadership—Moral and ethical aspects.   2. Leadership—Religious aspects.   I. Deal, Terrence E.   II. Title.
  HD57.7.B64 2011
  658.4'092—dc22

                                                                    2011014358

Printed in the United States of America
THIRD EDITION
HB Printing 10 9 8 7 6 5 4 3 2 1

For

Barry Edwin Deal
August 17, 1959–November 28, 1964

Robert Louis Deal
February 17, 1916–October 25, 2003

Dorothy Frances Deal
December 21, 1919–January 29, 2010

Eldred Ross Bolman
March 3, 1914–May 4, 1985

Florence Bernice Bolman
August 26, 1915–June 28, 1999

CONTENTS

CONTENTS

Leading

with

Soul

Prelude

In Search of Soul and Spirit

All day I think about it, then at night I say it.
Where did I come from,
and what am I supposed to be doing?
I have no idea.
My soul is from elsewhere, I'm sure of that,
and I intend to end up there

—Rumi

Soul. Spirit. The words sometimes sound strange to the modern ear. We rarely think or talk about where we came from or what we are here to do. But soul and spirit are vital companions whenever we ask what life is about and where our path is taking us. This book invites you to embark on a journey in search of meaning and purpose in a world gone crazy. In recent years we've all been stunned by one psychic shock after another. The horror of 9/11 and the age of perpetual terror that it signaled. The greenhouse effect, raising the specter that the energy we use to fuel civilization may eventually destroy it. A parade of business scandals—Enron, WorldCom, AIG, Madoff, BP's oil spill, the subprime mortgage debacle, and many more—making it hard to shake the belief that business leaders are short-sighted moral pygmies. The economic collapse of 2008 that shattered hope for people around the world and left millions haunted by fear and economic insecurity. A world adrift and out of control cries out for belief, hope, and inspired action.

Answering that poignant call for enlightenment and leadership at work is the goal of this book. It is a guide to the path we need to follow to find answers to questions none of us can escape. What can we hold on to? Where do we find solid footing? How can we create a better life and a better world? When each of us plunges into the depths of our being, there we find soul, a bedrock sense of identity and meaning—who we are, what we care about, and what we are here to do. We also discover spirit, a transcendent universal sense of oneness.

Soul and spirit are related in the same way as peaks and valleys, male and female. They are intimately connected. Each needs the other. The two are so interconnected that the words are often used interchangeably, but we see an important distinction. Soul is personal and unique, grounded in the depths of individual experience. Spirit is transcendent and all embracing. It is the universal source, the oneness of all things. Adherents of the world's great religions name it Allah, Brahman, the Buddha, God, or Jahweh. Others find this source in love, nature, humanity, magic, or an ineffable sense of oneness with the cosmos. One clue to the universality of spirit is its recurrence as a central source of power and possibility in many of history's most popular films. In *Star Wars,* it is called "the force," in *Lord of the Rings,* it is "the One," the remote creator, Eru Iluvatar. In *The Matrix,* "the One" is personified as Neo. In *Avatar,* as in many cultural traditions, spirit is pantheistic—God is in everything.

Soul and spirit are rooted in hope and faith—the things we believe even if they cannot be proven. Hope is the faith that dies last, the stubborn belief in new possibilities and a better tomorrow. Too often today's travails leave us in an existential void. We have a haunting sense that somewhere along the line we got off track. We're working harder than ever, but we're not really sure why. We feel a vague emptiness as we rush madly through life, hoping that we can escape if we keep running. Deep down, we fear we're losing the race. The need to reinfuse life at work with spirit, passion, and zest is greater than ever. "As millions of Americans arrive at their place of employment, the unfortunate reality is that many see their work environment not as an opportunity, but as a place of mundane misery."[1] Work satisfaction among American workers in 2009 reached the lowest level ever recorded. "It says something troubling about work in America. It is not about the business cycle or one grumpy generation," says Linda Barrington of the Conference Board, which sponsored the survey. Our spiritual malaise and longing for something more need to be filled with spirit and faith. Those are the gifts that leaders with soul bring to organizations.

The Spiritual Path

The search for soul and spirit is a quest for depth, meaning, and faith transcending boundaries of gender, age, geography, and race. It's as fresh and specific to our time as the latest high-tech gadget. It's a counterforce to the modern technical mind-set that can toss people into orbit and put a smartphone in every pocket, yet provides few answers for bringing joy to life, meaning to work, or integrity and conviction to leadership.

This movement travels an age-old path that is not confined to religious or mystical traditions. Atheists and Muslims, Christians and Humanists, Agnostics, Buddhists, and many more all embark on the same quest. They see different things along the way, but all seek answers to the same fundamental spiritual questions that are basic to being human. Even the rationalism that governs much of managerial thinking serves for some as a spiritual anchor. The view that people and organizations are essentially rational entities that respond to incentives is a powerful tool in managerial practice. It also serves as a theology for many adherents, but one that is often unfulfilling because it cuts believers off from soul and spirit.

Our approach is inclusive, open to all these perspectives and more. If you arrive deeply committed to your religious faith, join us on the journey. If you are convinced that the idea of God is absurd or traditional religion is mere superstition, we welcome you as well. Regardless of where you begin, we honor your search and seek to support it. Our goal is not to teach a specific theology or philosophy but to pose questions and stimulate reflection to help you deepen the faith you have or find the one you need. We invite you to become a coauthor.

Treat the stories and ideas in these pages as a stimulus and a starting point. Fill in the gaps you find in what we have produced by writing your own story and exploring your own path. Look for opportunities to share your reflections and questions with others. We hope the book can guide you on the journey of the soul that is vital to building inspired and inspiring leadership.

Over the centuries, people have found meaning in work, family, community, and shared belief. They have drawn upon shared resources to do what they could not do alone. United efforts—raising a barn, shoring up a levee, rescuing earthquake victims, celebrating a marriage, or singing a hymn—have brought people together, created enduring bonds, and exemplified the possibilities in collective spirit. Such traditional sources of meaning, energy, and achievement are increasingly endangered in a world of fleeting, virtual relationships. Individuals ponder a question posed two thousand years ago: What does it profit us if we gain the world but lose our souls?[2] It is no surprise that signs of spiritual hunger and restlessness are everywhere. Many of us brought hope and optimism into the new millennium only to find that almost all our certitudes failed. It is time to embark on a journey to seek answers to the questions that Rumi posed at the beginning of this chapter. Where did we come from? What are we here to do? What is the meaning of our life? What is our destiny?

Soulful Leadership

We hope that this book will stimulate a journey in search of your leadership gifts. Each of us has a special contribution to make if we can shoulder the personal and spiritual work needed to discover and share our own gifts. Across sectors and levels, organizations are starved for the leadership they need. Leaders who have lost touch with their souls, who are confused and uncertain about their core values and beliefs, inevitably lose their way or sound an uncertain trumpet.

A growing movement seeks to recapture the essence that soul and spirit can bring to the modern workplace and its environment. As Matthew Fox writes: "Life and livelihood ought not to be separated but to flow from the same source, which is Spirit, for both life and livelihood are about Spirit. Spirit means life, and both life and livelihood are about living in depth, living with meaning, purpose, joy, and a sense of contribution to the greater community. A spirituality of work is about bringing life and livelihood back together again. And spirit with them."[3]

Leading with soul brings meaning and purpose back to workplaces that have lost them. It goes beyond technology, efficiency, and the bottom line to meet human needs for success and ful-fillment. Spirited leadership fires motivation, deepens loyalty, and galvanizes performance. It reinfuses soul and spirit, marry-ing the two so that spirit feeds soul and soul enriches spirit. Committed and passionate leaders find their soul's treasure store and offer its gifts to others.[4]

The chapters ahead explore why soul, spirit, faith, and hope belong at the heart of leadership. They do this through a dia-logue between a beleaguered leader and a wise sage. Over the centuries, spiritual leaders of all traditions and faiths have taught and learned through example, story, and dialogue. Sufi and Christian parables, Zen koans, the Jewish Haggadah, Hindu legends, and Native American stories are but a few examples. In our story, you are invited to join Steve Camden, a highly suc-cessful, fast-track manager who has run into an existential wall, as he works with Maria, a spiritual mentor.

Our Journey

This book began as a product of providence rather than plan-ning. It was an unexpected calling that emerged during an informal lunch with colleagues at our publisher, Jossey-Bass. We arrived that day with a list of potential book projects, all well within our social science comfort zone. Partway through the

meeting, Lynn Luckow, then president of Jossey-Bass, interrupted the conversation's flow to ask a simple, inspired question:
"What do you really want to do? Blue-sky it." Silence fell over
the breaking of bread and sipping of wine as we both gradually
realized the awful truth: we didn't know what we really wanted
to do. Out of that silence came a surprising reply: "We'd like to
do a book about leadership and spirit." (Thanks again, Lynn, for
being the godfather of this project.)

That answer put us on an unfamiliar and scary path. We had
committed to write a book with only a hazy idea of where we
were going and what we had to say. Fortunately, many friends
and colleagues came to our rescue with ideas and support. We
plunged into the great spiritual literature from around the world:
the Tao, the Koran, the Bible, the Bhagavad-Gita, Sufi poetry,
Native American mythology, African American folk tales, the
Tibetan Book of the Dead, and many other works. All these
helped greatly, but they were not enough. We also had to go
deep inside to find our own spiritual centers. We couldn't write
about anyone else's spiritual journey without examining and
deepening our own. We couldn't talk about soul and spirit
without experiencing firsthand what they meant for us.

For Terry, this journey triggered a conversation with his wife,
Sandy, that eventually led him to give up a tenured position at

Vanderbilt University so that he and Sandy could fulfill their dream of returning home to California to design and build a house on the central coast. It also enabled him to revisit a painful chapter in his life that he had neglected for many years—the tragic death in 1964 of his five-year-old son Barry. The impact on Lee was equally profound—difficult but essential reappraisals of a painful divorce and the death of his father, a recommitment to religious faith, and a move to Kansas City and the University of Missouri after more than twenty years at Harvard University.

This story is a parable drawn from our own lives and the lives of others we have known. We hope it speaks to you. To assist your reflections, we punctuate the story with a series of interludes—meditations on the issues and questions raised in the story. Walt Whitman captures our hopes for your journey:

> Sail forth—steer for the deep waters only,
> Reckless O soul, exploring, I with thee,
>   and thou with me,
> For we are bound where mariner has not yet
>   dared to go,
> And we will risk the ship, ourselves and all.[5]

The Search

CHAPTER 1

The Heart of Leadership Lives in the Hearts of Leaders

He was tired, and it was getting dark. He'd driven three hours up mountain roads. Not by choice. Why had John sent him? Who was this woman he was supposed to meet? He didn't know, and didn't like not knowing. He liked to read a review before seeing a movie or reading a book.

His name was Steven Camden. Like the city in New Jersey. He grew up in New Jersey, but in Newark, not Camden. Not that it made much difference. Tough neighborhoods in both places. He'd survived one of the toughest.

The house was low, made of wood and glass. A candle flickering in a window. *Faux rustic or Asian or something,* he thought. He bounded up the maple-leaf-matted fieldstone steps at his usual brisk pace, but he felt more puzzled than confident.

He knocked on the door. He waited. Was she here? She knew he was coming, didn't she? She must know he had better things to do than just stand on her doorstep. Hadn't John told her how busy he is? He looked again and she was there.

Her name was Maria. He first noticed her eyes: deep,

brown, full of something he recognized but could not name. Once inside, he looked around the room. Mostly he noticed the Japanese art. It was like a gallery. Yet something was missing.

You've spent time in Japan, he said.

She nodded. Many years. Every piece is a memory.

I lived in Tokyo two years myself. For him, Tokyo had been endless business meetings. No time for galleries. His only souvenirs came from the airport duty-free shop.

She seemed to be waiting.

Was he supposed to make the next move? Where to begin? Blurt out his worries to a woman he barely knew? He tried to buy time. John seems to have a lot of confidence in you, he said.

We're old friends. I knew him back when he was starting the business. We've become even closer since he retired. I've learned a lot from him.

She seemed to be waiting again. Now what? He'd always been good with words. Where were they now?

Do you feel uncomfortable here? she asked.

No. He hesitated. Well, maybe a little. Maybe I shouldn't have come.

Have some tea.

He watched her pour the tea. He wanted coffee, but took the tea.

You've been working hard?

All my life. He sipped his tea. Green tea. Reminded him of Japan. He'd ordered it many times. *Nihon cha, kudasai.* A comforting sense of nostalgia.

Why? she asked.

Why what? He'd lost track.

Why do you work so hard?

He paused. What kind of question was that? Why does anyone work hard? It's what you do. It's how I got where I am.

Do you like where you are?

Of course. He was lying. He knew it. Did she? Probably. Well, maybe not. Not as much as I used to.

What's changed?

He hesitated. Was he walking into a trap? Should he leave? Or tell the truth? He vaguely imagined John looking over his shoulder. *Why be scared of this woman?* he wondered. Then, a second thought. *What do I have to lose?*

I was promoted a year ago. Running one of our biggest divisions. I was sure I was ready.

And now?

He stared at the cranes delicately circling the outside of his teacup. Until he met this woman, he liked to think nothing scared him. He hesitated.

I'm not sure.

What's changed?

Until this job, everything went right. People thought I could walk on water. Maybe it was talent, maybe luck, maybe just a lot of sweat. Something's not working anymore. He looked down and signaled his puzzlement by exhaling loudly.

You're discouraged? She sounded sincere. Why did she make him so nervous?

Like I'm on a treadmill. Running faster and faster. Getting farther and farther behind.

You need to get off.

I didn't need to drive three hours to learn that. He knew he sounded impatient. That's how he felt.

What have you tried?

Just about everything. Better time management. A mission statement. Strategic planning. Balanced scorecard. Training. A Six Sigma program.

Why was she staring at him? Why so silent? Did she think he'd done the wrong things? That he hadn't done enough?

He continued. I've sent executives to a top-rated management program. Hired consultants. World-class guys with world-class fees. I read a lot. The *Journal*. *Fortune*. *Harvard Business Review*. Industry blogs, but that's mostly a waste of time.

She laughed. Why do you do all those things?

Her laughter grated. He felt his shoulders tighten. Was she laughing at him?

It worked before. Why not now?

She turned serious. What do you want from me?

The question stung. What did he really want? He wasn't sure. He groped for an answer. His mouth felt dry.

My work is my life. Always has been. I grew up poor, and I didn't want to stay that way. Now, I've got money but a lot of the fun is gone. My boss is getting restless. First time I ever felt I might fail in a job.

What's not working? she asked.

He told her about needing unity, but people never agreeing. He said he needed a vision, but it was hard to see beyond next week. Things seemed to be falling apart. He was losing hope. He'd never felt so lost.

She said she'd been there. That she understood.

Where had she been? Did she really understand? He wanted to say something. No words came.

And your spirit? she asked.

He looked to the door. He wanted to run. Get some fresh air. Get away from this crazy woman. Somehow, he couldn't move. Spirit? he stammered.

Yes, your spirit. Her tone was firm, assured. As if it were a perfectly normal question. Was she serious?

What do you mean?

Spirit. Fire. Vitality. The force that sustains meaning and hope.

He was squirming. Was it a mistake for him to come?

A business is what you make it, she said calmly. If you believe it's a machine, it will be. A temple? It can be that too. Spirit and faith are the core of human life. Without them, you lose your way. You live without zest. You go through the motions, but don't know why.

He felt the anger building. He'd driven three hours for this? Teeth clenched, he told her what he felt. Look, I'm running a business, not a church! He sounded angry. He meant to. It usually made people back off.

But not this time. Her eyes riveted on his. She smiled. What do you hope to run it with? More sweat? More control? More gimmicks?

Maybe some wisdom. He hadn't meant to say that, but it came out anyway.

Wisdom will come. First, you have to look into your heart.

He was squirming again. Embarrassed. He could feel the blood rushing to his face. Why was he still here? Why didn't he get up and walk out? You sound like my mother, he said scornfully. Follow your heart, she always said. She never understood business.

Do you? she asked.

Of course.

Then, set a new course. You want to lead, don't you?

He nodded glumly.

She continued. The heart of leadership is in the hearts of leaders. You have to lead from something deep inside.

Like what?

I can't tell you what's in your heart, nor would you want me to. No one can find meaning for you. Not your consultants, not your boss, not the *Harvard Business Review*. Only you really know what's in your heart.

He felt a twinge in his chest. A coincidence? He knew he'd been working too hard.

This isn't what you expected, she said.

Not at all.

It feels strange?

She was right. He wanted to be in control, but she was running a step ahead of him.

Maybe a little, he admitted, wishing he hadn't.

She poured him more tea. You've been in uncomfortable situations before, haven't you?

Sure.

Have you learned from them?

He tried to review all his awkward moments. He gave up. There had been too many. Usually.

Good. Then, shall we continue?

Continue what? A senseless conversation? Still, she seemed to be onto something. Something he sensed but couldn't grasp. Maybe. I'm not sure.

Would you like some time to reflect? A walk, maybe?

His phone rang. He felt embarrassed. I told my secretary only to call only if it's important.

Take the call. Then the walk. Try the garden. We'll talk more when you get back.

CHAPTER 2

The Human Heart Is More Than a Pump

The walk helped. A chance to clear his head. He'd heard she was good. Very good. But she wasn't making sense. Off in the ozone. Talk more, she'd said. About what? How could he get her on his wavelength?

He found her reading in her study. Look, he said. I've thought it over. Heart and spirit can wait. I've got problems now!

She looked up from her book. You're missing the point.

His jaw tightened. He was tired of playing games. He spat out, What the hell are you talking about?

You. She paused, looking at him. You're decisive. You get things done.

Yeah. *She's starting to get it,* he thought.

You think things through. You're a good analyst.

True.

You take charge. You're on top of things.

One of my strengths. He was feeling better now. She was beginning to understand him.

Maybe your biggest weakness.

Was this a trick? He hated weakness. He felt his face flush again. He could barely control his rage.

Look, I'm a manager, not a social worker. You've got to be tough to get ahead.

She ignored the anger in his voice. How tough?

Why couldn't she get it? Put her in her place, then get out of here. John said you could help. Obviously bad advice. You're off the mark. Wasting my time. You're . . .

She laughed gently. At him?

I'm sorry, he said. I don't mean to offend you. Why was he apologizing? She should feel sorry for being useless.

Are you trying to scare me away? she asked.

She was right. She was getting too close. He knew the pattern. When you feel vulnerable, go on the attack. It usually worked.

OK, I'm upset. I'm tired. I'm looking for help.

Maybe your head and hands have taken you as far as they can.

Suppose that's true. Then what?

Try a new route. A journey of the heart.

A journey of the heart? Sounds like a TV soap opera.

Your heart is more than a pump. It's your spiritual center. It's courage and compassion. If you lose heart, life is empty, lonely. You're always occupied but never fulfilled.

He felt panicky. He wanted to protest but couldn't find the words. Then it hit him. Right in the pit of his stomach. *Maybe she's right.*

You've had a long day, she said.

He nodded.

Get some rest. We'll talk more in the morning.

CHAPTER 3

The Journey of a Soul

They followed a path curving gently up the mountainside. Above, a canopy of pine and spruce filtered the morning sun. Below, a blanket of wildflowers and a lake. *Beautiful,* he thought. The smells and sounds of spring surrounded them.

I love it here, she said.

I can see why. Maybe I should get out more often. He couldn't remember his last walk in the woods. Too little time. Too much to do.

If you let it, nature lifts your spirit. It touches your heart.

Spirit. Heart. Again. What was she trying to tell him?

Does this journey of the heart come with a road map? he asked.

It's an inward journey. There's no map. You find your soul by looking deep within. There you discover your spiritual center.

I'm looking for something more concrete.

How can I give you directions to your soul?

Are you a therapist?

No.

Some kind of religious nut?

She laughed. Does the word *soul* scare you?

No, no. He was nervous. Puzzled. Not scared. It's just that I didn't come here for sermons. I want answers.

Are you finding them?

No. Why do you think I'm here? He felt his annoyance rising again.

An old sage was once walking along a path very much like this one. A man, not much younger than you, approached from the other direction. The young man's eyes were so riveted to the path that he bumped into the sage. The sage looked at the young man sternly and asked him where he was going. "To catch my future," the young man replied. "How do you know you haven't already passed it?" the sage asked.

You're talking about me.

Do you think so?

He hated to admit it, but yes.
Eyes front. Tunnel vision. He
was conceding more than
he wanted.

She didn't seem
surprised by his admis-
sion. Same Mona Lisa
expression. Same warm, soft tone.
A journey of the soul is a quest
through uncharted territory. You
find your way by opening your
eyes. And your heart.

A ground squirrel scam-
pered across the path. It
seemed to know where it was
going. Why didn't he?

So, if I believe what you're telling me, where do
I begin? he asked.

Where you are.

I'm not sure where that is.

That's a good beginning.

For what?

Your journey.

What if I'm not in a mood for traveling?

You're not. She paused. You won't be for a while.

Why?

Because you're starting to realize that what you're looking for is on the path you're afraid of taking.

He'd never considered it before, but deep-down he knew she was right.

They came to a stream and sat down in silence. A leaf floated past.

CHAPTER 4

Discovering New Teachers

See that leaf. It wends its way to wherever the stream takes it.

Look, I'm not a leaf. He meant to sound forceful. I'm a manager. My job is to control things, not just float with the current.

She moved closer. Looked directly at him. Her eyes felt penetrating. Control is an illusion. It's seductive because it gives a feeling of power. Something to hold on to. So it becomes addictive. It's hard to give up even when it's not working. You can't start a journey until you let go of habits holding you back.

Tell it to my boss. I'm paid to be in charge.

That's the illusion. Look again at the water going by. There is a story about a stream that flowed around many obstacles until it arrived at a desert. The stream tried to cross, but its waters disappeared into the sand.

What's this got to do with me?

Maybe you and the stream have something in common.

Well, he snorted, neither of us seems to be getting anywhere at the moment.

And neither of you wants to change. In the past, you always got past obstacles. Now you're trying to cross a desert. But you don't know how.

That's a stretch. But if the stream found any answers, fill me in. I haven't heard any since I got here.

She ignored his sarcasm. The stream heard a voice. It said, "The wind crosses the desert. So can the stream." The stream protested, "The wind can fly but I cannot." The voice responded, "Let yourself be absorbed by the wind." The stream rebelled. "I want to remain the same stream I am today." "Not possible," said the voice. "But your essence, your ultimate character, can be carried away and become a stream again. You've forgotten your essence." The stream remembered dimly that she had once been held in the wind. She let her vapor rise into the arms of the wind, which carried it across the desert and

then let it fall in the mountains.
There it again became
a stream.

Evaporation
won't work for
me.

But
letting go
might.

Letting go of
what?

The
defenses
you're using to

push me away. The mind-set that's got you stuck.

He looked away. He stared at the stream for several minutes.
Let go. Of what? Of something he had clutched tightly for too
long. He watched another leaf, trying to hold back the feelings
welling up. They came anyway.

He spoke slowly, his voice cracking.

In the story, the stream remembered a time long before when
the wind had held it. Being held in the past. He hesitated,
waiting for a wave of feelings to pass. I was five when my father

died. Sweetest guy in the world. Never stayed in a job. Left me and my mom with nothing. We didn't talk about him much. The message was always, "Don't be like him. Make something of yourself."

Have you followed that advice?

It worked. At least I thought so.

So you've been trying not to be your father. Making sure you're not the sweetest guy in the world?

He looked down and swallowed hard, trying to get on top of a wave of feelings. Was he angry? Sad? Or just confused? It sounds crazy, he finally said, but yes. I loved my dad. Still miss him, but I've been trying to be everything he wasn't. Maybe I have lost something. Somewhere along the way.

You've rejected what you loved in your father.

Steve felt blind. How did I go so long without seeing that?

You've been running from yourself. You lost touch with your soul.

If that's true, where do I look?

Inside. Outside. Your soul is inside, at your core. Teachers can help you find it.

Which teachers?

They're all around you.

Been to dozens of seminars. Workshops. Taught by top people. I didn't always learn that much.

Did any of them mention soul?

No. They usually don't. Not in management seminars.

She laughed. At least she had a sense of humor.

You're looking in the wrong places, she said. Life's deepest lessons are often where you least expect them.

Like the school of hard knocks.

Sometimes the lessons are very hard. I remember a man who met regularly with a group of friends. One day, he said to his friends, "I have discovered a new teacher. It's called pancreatic cancer."

The story cut deep. Beyond his usual defenses. He tried to dam the emotion coming from somewhere deep inside. Don't cry, he told himself. The tears came anyway. His face reddened with embarrassment. Why was he crying in front of this woman he barely knew?

It's a powerful story, she said softly. His friends cried too. Their tears almost hid the real lesson. On life's journey, we pass guideposts every day. Mostly we don't notice. Tragedy is the author of hope.

He struggled to stop the tears, but they kept coming. She waited until he was able to speak.

I watched my mom die of melanoma. It's a slow, ugly way to die. Worst experience of my life. Even worse than my dad's death. Or my divorce. I was devastated.

Are you still?

Maybe.

Were you her hope?

That's what she used to tell me.

Loss can bring you face to face with your soul.

He shook his head. I just threw myself into my work. Maybe I missed something.

You postponed it. It's still waiting for you on your journey.

Soul. Journey. He spoke deliberately, pondering each word. Not so long ago, I'd have been out of here.

And now?

Reclaiming Your Soul

*It is by going into the abyss that we recover the
treasures of life.*

Where you stumble, there lies your treasure.

*The very cave you are afraid to enter turns out to
be the source of what you are looking for. The
damned thing in the cave that was so dreaded has
become the center. You find the jewel and it draws
you off.*[1]

—Joseph Campbell

In their very first meeting, Maria invites Steve Camden to plunge into his own personal abyss. Sensibly enough, he hesitates. Does this crazy woman have any idea what she is talking about? Will the cave he is afraid to enter really bring him to what he is seeking? Or will that "damned thing in the cave" simply bring more pain and confusion? Is this trip necessary, or might it be a gigantic waste of time? Steve hopes Maria will provide an itinerary and travel insurance before he takes the plunge. She declines, knowing she can invite and encourage but cannot tell him what will happen on his odyssey or protect him from its rigors.

The malaise that has brought Steve Camden to Maria is widely shared. Albert Schweitzer called it a "sleeping sickness of the soul."[2] Its symptoms are loss of seriousness, enthusiasm, and zest. When we live superficially, pursue no goals deeper than material success, and ignore our inner voices, we stunt our spiritual development. Today's stressful and turbulent world compounds our risk of shrunken souls and spiritual malaise. Technology—in the form of social networking sites like Facebook and Twitter, and dating sites like eHarmony—has become the primary means many of us use to connect with others. We can link instantly to people across the street or around the world via tweets and instant messages, only to reap an endless series of brief and superficial encounters. We link proudly to hundreds or even thousands of acquaintances, but we know few of them well and sacrifice quality for quantity, depth for breadth. As Robert Putnam warned, we wind up severed from family, community, and ourselves, because we've substituted digital surfing for human engagement.[3] Robert Lane marshals evidence of a long-term decline in happiness in prosperous democratic societies. He argues that more and more of us are misled by a materialist culture to put money and possessions at the center of our lives. We swallow the bait, ignoring the growing evidence that people who focus their lives on tangible goods are demonstrably less happy than people who strive for other, deeper purposes.[4]

The resulting restlessness and discontent inevitably leak into workplaces. Managers try almost anything to stay current and make their organizations successful. Sometimes their efforts pay off. Too often they and their organizations lose touch with their core identity—their soul. This is true despite research showing that companies with a nucleus of beliefs and values transcending the bottom line are, paradoxically, more profitable over time than companies focused only on making money.[5]

As consultants and researchers, we have repeatedly found that managers' first response to any situation is to focus on its rational and technical features. Analyze. Plan. Change policies. Restructure. Reengineer. For many business problems, these are sensible responses, but they miss another, deeper dimension. The symbolic, expressive facets of organizational life are at the heart of inspired leadership. Have we merely rediscovered cha-risma, the label often given to leaders endowed with mystery, magic, or a gift from the gods? Or are we seeing something deeper than that? Warren Buffett, one of America's most respected business leaders, once said that he looked for three qualities in new hires: integrity, intelligence, and energy. Hire someone without the first, he added, and the other two will kill you.[6] We've seen the truth of his observation too many times in both business and politics. The leaders who brought Enron to catas-trophe were proud of being "the smartest guys in the room," but lacked integrity and ethical guardrails to bound their intelli-gence and ambition. Integrity is rooted in identity and faith, which are at the heart of authentic leadership.

In Search of Soul

It is often said that people today need a new paradigm to move beyond the traps of conventional thinking. In truth, we may need to rediscover and renew an old paradigm, one deeply embedded in traditional wisdom. Steve Camden, this story's embattled leader, is lost. With the help of a spiritual guide, he is starting along a new path. Instead of looking outside for techniques and recipes, he will learn to look inward for a deeper source of wisdom. As John the Evangelist wrote to the early Christians about their understanding of Jesus, "The spirit you have received from him remains within you, and you don't need to have any man teach you. But that spirit teaches you all things and is the truth."[7] The same message is found in many other spiritual traditions. In a story from eighth-century China, a novice went to Ma-tzu, a spiritual master, in search of the Buddha's teaching. Ma-tzu asked him why he sought help from others when he already had the greatest treasure inside him. The novice asked what treasure he meant, and Ma-tzu replied: "Where is your question coming from? This is your treasure. It is precisely what is asking the question at this very moment. Everything is stored in this precious treasure-house of yours. It is there at your wish. Nothing is lacking. Why, then, are you running away from yourself and seeking for things outside?"[8]

The twenty-first-century milieu puts many obstacles in the way of this pilgrimage to our spiritual center. Our entrenched pragmatic orientation places a premium on technical logic. Our tendency to specialize and compartmentalize leads us to sever work and play, male and female, career and family, thinking and feeling, reason and spirit. We relegate spirituality to churches, temples, and mosques—for those who still attend them. We shun it at work. To change this way of thinking is far from easy, but more and more of us are recognizing the costs of the separation.

One of the principal findings of Mitroff and Denton's landmark study of spirituality in the workplace was that *"people do not want to compartmentalize or fragment their lives. The search for meaning, purpose, wholeness, and integration is a constant, never-ending task. To confine this search to one day a week or after hours violates people's basic sense of integrity, of being whole persons. In short, soul is not something one leaves at home."*[9]

Steve's encounter with Maria has put him on the verge of a perilous existential journey. Early on, he will rely heavily on his spiritual guide for support and direction. Yet she will resist his efforts to put her in charge. Instead, she affirms a message found in almost every major spiritual tradition: Don't ask someone else to take control of your spiritual journey. Instead, recognize and trust the power within you to seek, reflect, and find.

Steve will learn that his task is to reclaim and rekindle his spiritual center. What he needs to find is already within him because spirit is unquenchable. "It does not matter how long

your spirit lies dormant and unused. One day you hear a song, look at an object, or see a vision and you feel its presence. It can't be bought, traded, or annihilated, because its power comes from its story. No one can steal your spirit. You have to give it away. You can also take it back."[10] Yet taking it back is rarely easy. Steve is embarking on a voyage of self-discovery that he has avoided for years. He will need to overcome his fears of what he might find by looking within. He cannot know in advance how much pain, emptiness, or terror he will have to face—nor what reserves of courage and wisdom he will discover to sustain him along the way.

The Spiritual Journey

His quest will be filled with paradox. "Spirituality transcends the ordinary; and yet, paradoxically, it can be found only in the ordinary. Spirituality is beyond us and yet is in everything we do. It is extraordinary, and yet it is extraordinarily simple."[11]

Another paradox is that the specifics of each person's journey can never be forecast, even though the journey's outlines are known to us all. This quest is the most often told tale in all human cultures. The ancients told this epic story centuries ago, and it endures today among our most popular best sellers.

The *Odyssey,* some three thousand years old, tells the story of the warrior king Odysseus, who must journey for years struggling to overcome treacherous enemies, human foibles, and the whims of the Gods before he can finally return home. *Beowulf,* one of the oldest surviving works in English literature, tells of a prince, Beowulf, who establishes his leadership by courageously going forth to confront and destroy a murderous beast, Grendel. Beowulf soon learns the price of victory: he must face Grendel's vicious and vengeful mother in her den at the bottom of an icy pond. The English poet David Whyte has explored the spiritual message in the story. In going to the depths to confront Grendel's mother, Whyte tells us, Beowulf is in quest of his own soul. Symbolically, Grendel's mother represents the beast within himself that Beowulf must face and conquer if he is to know himself and to grow.[12]

Fast-forward to the twenty-first century and we still clamor for new versions of the same story. Though they do not always fare well with literary critics, three of the biggest-selling authors of the twenty-first century, Dan Brown and Stephenie Meyer (with more than 100 million books sold apiece) and J. K. Rowling (with more than 400 million sales), have each created a pop-culture sensation with a series of novels and feature films that provide distinctive takes on the hero's journey. The hero may be a Harvard professor of religious symbols (in Brown's *The Da Vinci Code*), a dreamy teenage heroine struggling to survive a love/hate relationship with vampires (in Meyer's *Twilight* trilogy), or an English boy wizard (in Rowling's *Harry Potter* series). But in each case, the hero must leave home, embark on a perilous journey into the unknown that puts both life and soul at risk, find the courage and wisdom to survive, and return home with skills and strengths earned on the quest.

None of these heroes, from Odysseus to *Twilight's* Bella, is foolish enough to go alone on the quest. Beowulf is aided by loyal retainers. Bella is protected and supported by friends and allies. The challenges and dangers of the spiritual journey are so great that few are likely to succeed without help. Steve Camden will need the guide he has found in Maria to support him along the way. As authors, neither of us could have written *Leading with Soul* alone. We needed each other's support and counsel as we sought our own spiritual centers.

In *Beowulf, Twilight,* and the countless other variations on the story of spiritual development, the hero's journey typically moves through three major stages. The first stage is leaving home—often physically but especially psychically and spiritually. Leaving home requires letting go of comfortable and familiar ways. It makes it possible to escape the shackles of established convention and everyday routine. In his very first meeting with Maria, Steve begins to take this initial step—letting go of the old psychic anchors and entrenched defenses that have locked him into a particular way of thinking about himself and his life. As is often the case in such journeys, Steve leaves home not because he wants to but because he has to. He has hit a brick wall—his old patterns and assumptions have been failing him. He has tried to get around the wall by doing more of what he knows, but that has also failed. Because home has become intolerable, Steve is willing to risk embarking on a new journey.

Leaving home leads to the journey's second stage—the quest. The quest is a time of almost overwhelming danger and challenge. Beowulf and Bella both narrowly avert death. Steve, like most modern managers, faces only trivial physical dangers. But he correctly recognizes that the psychological and spiritual stakes are high. That is why his initial impulse is to reject the journey—to "get away from this crazy woman." That urge will return from time to time, because the quest has peaks and valleys, straightaways and convoluted turns. Only if he persists will Steve Camden be ready for the third stage of the journey, returning home. Home will be different and so will he, because he will be armed with new capacities and the deeper understanding that he could acquire only by undertaking this journey.

As Joseph Campbell said: "The dark night of the soul comes just before revelation. When everything is lost, and all seems darkness, then comes the new life and all that is needed."[13] But at the moment, most of the adventure still lies ahead for Steve Camden. Like Beowulf and Bella, he will find that reclaiming his soul requires uncommon courage and persistence.

Conviction

CHAPTER 5

A Place to Start

A month had passed. He was back on her doorstep. Waiting again. His shoulders were slumped, his expression dour. He felt his heart pounding. Where was she? Why was he back? He knew something had pulled him, but he wasn't sure what. Finally she was there. He felt better. She hadn't deserted him.

She led him to her study. Motioned him to a chair.

He sat down. Groped for words that wouldn't come.

How are you doing? she asked.

Looking for insights. Waiting for a light bulb to go on.

And?

Nothing. Darkness. More confusion. He looked down. He felt stupid.

That's good.

He was surprised. Why good?

Signs you've begun your journey. You start from where you are. At the beginning, confusion is normal.

But I feel lost.

That's why you can't just stay where you are.

How can I move on if I don't know where I am or where I'm going?

You want everything planned in advance. That's fine for a trip to Chicago. It won't work for a journey of the spirit. First, you have to get started. Move into uncharted territory. Explore. Reflect. You'll know when you're on course.

It feels like a leap.

It is. That's the point.

How do I know the landing won't be painful?

It probably will be.

Not a very persuasive sales pitch.

Do you have a better option?

I wouldn't be here if I did.

Then talk about what scares you.

Did I say I was scared?

Isn't that why you want me to guarantee a comfortable trip?

He didn't like to admit it, but he knew she was right. A memory from childhood came back. I got lost at a carnival once.

I was panicked. Terrified. I still dream about it. Remember Hansel and Gretel? In new places, I still leave crumbs.

She was smiling broadly. Almost beaming.

What's so funny? he asked.

I'm smiling because I have my own stories of being terrified. As a little girl, I used to play in a field next to our house. It was hot one summer. Everything was very dry. I built a campfire. It jumped over the ring of rocks. The whole field caught fire. It took the fire department two hours to put it out. I felt stupid. For a long time, I was terrified of doing the wrong thing again. I tried to avoid anything risky.

That's not what I've heard about you.

I've learned on my journey. I wanted to find courage—like the Cowardly Lion in *The Wizard of Oz*. The Wizard says that everyone is afraid. Courage is the ability to go on anyway. It took me a long time, but I've learned to push ahead despite fear.

I want you to be the wizard. Give me the answers.

Zen masters often say that if you see a teacher coming, chase her away.

Why? That sounds crazy.

If you discover something within, no one can hide it from you. If you haven't, no one can find it for you.

You keep telling me to look inside. When I do, I hear the same voices. *Be rational. Be in control. Be careful.* You're hearing from your head, not your heart. It's hard to let go of old patterns. It takes courage and faith.

Where do I find them?

You keep looking.

Where?

She stood up and waved him over to a window. Those woods up the hill go for miles. Take a walk. Get off the path. Explore. Make sure of one thing. Get lost.

Get lost? He stared at her in disbelief.

Exactly. Try it. See what happens.

I already know. I panic.

You think you know. You might discover something else. The Buddha began his journey by leaving the comforts of home and going where he'd never been. In the legend of the Holy Grail, each knight began his search by entering the darkest place in the forest. No path. No guide.

He started toward the door. He hesitated. Old fears pulled at him.

She watched him turn around.

This feels strange. Like a big step off the edge.

It is.

He smiled. Any crumbs to leave along the way?

They both laughed as he headed out the door.

CHAPTER 6

Vicissitudes of the Journey

It was getting dark. He was still lost, scrambling down a brushy slope. He never saw the branch until it slapped him in the face. It stung. His eyes watering, he sat down. He fought the panic. Old memories swept over him. His father's death. His mother's illness. Living with grandparents. Working his way through college. Vowing to be successful. Getting what he wanted. Finding that it only brought more worries.

Much later, he was back at her house, enjoying the aroma of fresh coffee.

I was about to mount a search party. She smiled.

Was she amused? Or relieved?

You told me to get lost. I did.

Do you ever do anything halfway? Then she noticed the blood. What happened?

Close encounter with a tree. It won.

Here. Let's clean it off.

It's nothing.

Sit down! She spoke sternly. I'll be back in a minute.

He protested weakly. She ignored him and washed the scrape. Her touch felt gentler than he expected. Close, her eyes were brighter, deeper. Like peering into a surging seascape. Should he let her get so close? His feelings were almost too intense. He looked away.

Found a lake, he said, trying to change the subject. Walked around it a couple of times. Ran into more than the branch. Discovered things I buried long ago.

You can learn a lot walking around a lake.

When you were young, did you learn a prayer, "Now I lay me down to sleep?"

She interrupted. "I pray the Lord my soul to keep."

The next lines terrified me. "If I should die before I wake, / I pray the Lord my soul to take." Particularly after my father died.

Do you still pray?

Not for years.

Why not?

Never seemed to make a difference. I stopped believing.

What do you believe in now?

I don't know. Work? Myself? Maybe nothing? He sounded resigned.

If you don't know what you believe in, you don't know who you are. Or why you're here. You can't see where you're going. She spoke slowly, quietly. Every word emphasized.

I used to know where I was going. I got lost somehow.

Prayer is one avenue to faith. A way to have an intimate conversation with your soul. A heartsong.

A heartsong?

A message from your heart. Your heart knows things that your mind can't. Heartsongs sustain you through the vicissitudes of the journey.

Vicissitudes? When had he last heard that word? In church? In the back of his mind a distant echo.

She continued. A spiritual pilgrimage brings peaks and valleys. A heartsong sustains you along the way.

I remember sitting with my mother in a black church. Music and singing. So much energy and intensity. Joy in the room.

But spirituals are about suffering as well as happiness. They're a way to survive the pain. Heartsongs carry us through both exhilaration and heartache.

Keep the heartache. I just want the exhilaration.

That's why you've etherized your life—to avoid the pain. At a price. If you wall off the valleys, you close off the peaks as well. It's better to stop and sing from time to time.

Ether. Pain. More memories. His divorce. His children's suffering. An older son who never forgave him. The feelings would wait no longer.

He felt her touch.

Fifteen years since my divorce, he said. My oldest son still doesn't answer my letters. The pain never stopped.

What did you do with it?

Ignored it. Threw myself into my work.

Did you talk to anyone?

A counselor. Not much help. I was trying to get to something. Something deeper. I never found it.

Good counselors know the psyche. Great ones know the soul. People used to go to their priest or rabbi for spiritual guidance. Now where do they go?

Nowhere, I guess. Just bury the feelings. Like I did.

You've suffered spiritual wounds. They're still not healed.

Is healing possible?

Yes. Not easy. But possible.

How?

Tragedy and loss enter every life. Spirit springs from what you make of them. Wounds provide an eye to see new possibilities.

He remembered a story. I had a friend who wanted to be a champion rock climber. He got trapped in the mountains for a couple of days. Frostbite. Both legs amputated below the knee. He was determined to climb again. He got artificial limbs for climbing. Someone asked him how he could climb so well. He laughed. He said now his calves didn't cramp.

She smiled. Humor is a wonderful heartsong.

I need to find my own.

Leaning Into Your Fear

The Courage of Conviction

A good traveler has no fixed plans and is not intent upon arriving. A good artist lets his intuition lead him wherever it wants. A good scientist has freed himself of concepts and keeps his mind open to what is.[1]

—Lao Tzu

Steve seeks help when he becomes frightened and hopeless. He prides himself on being a no-nonsense, get-it-done manager, so he insists on concrete solutions to immediate concerns. He resists seeing that his outward struggles are symptoms of something much deeper. Slowly, reluctantly, he begins to see that his real challenge is to come to terms with his soul. He begins to trust Maria as his guide.

Finding Our Spiritual Centers

The spiritual journey that we as leaders must take to inspire others begins *with* ourselves but not necessarily *by* ourselves. Maria asks Steve to look both inside and outside, because his quest will require both an inner exploration of soul and an external search for communion. To aid in the inner journey, every religious tradition has developed spiritual disciplines— exercises for getting in touch with something bigger. One is prayer, one form of the "heartsong" that Maria offered to Steve. Prayer, Ann and Barry Ulanov tell us, is primary speech. "[It] starts without words and often ends without them. . . . It works some of the time in signs and symbols, lurches when it must, leaps when it can, has several kinds of logic at its disposal."[2] Other spiritual disciplines include meditating, studying scriptures, singing hymns, following prescribed rituals, journeying to sacred places, and contemplating nature. Similar practices have evolved independently in many different places and eras. There is a meditative tradition, for example, in almost every major religion, including Buddhism, Christianity, Hinduism, Islam, and Judaism.

The external journey is a search for collective spirit, for true community with others. Steve has found a spiritual guide. He might have drawn support from a circle of friends, a spouse, a group of close colleagues, or a religious community. Whatever the source, the first step toward enlightenment is an exploration of our inner being, a search for our spiritual center. Only then can we lead others. As Eric Klein and John Izzo write in *Awakening Corporate Soul*, "In the end, it is not our techniques, our talents or our knowledge that matter, it is our being."[3]

Like many managers, Steve has been telling himself that nothing scares him—until he finds himself struggling to confront his fears of letting go, being out of control, or losing contact with comforting habitual anchors. He is beginning to embrace an ancient spiritual maxim: to hold too tightly to anything is to lose everything. Said a seventh-century Zen master: "The Great Way isn't difficult for those who are unattached to their preferences. Let go of longing and aversion, and everything will be perfectly clear."[4]

William Blake said it another way:

> He who binds himself to a joy
> Does the winged life destroy.
> But he who kisses the joy as it flies
> Lives in eternity's sun rise.[5]

Steve came to Maria because his confidence was eroding and his carefully constructed world was crumbling. His conversations with Maria are helping him find the determination to move on and open himself to new possibilities. He cannot know in advance where his quest will lead. The decision to begin and the conviction to persevere must rest on faith in the groping rather than foreknowledge of the grasp. The journey begins only when Steve's heart tells him that this is what he must do—even if reason and logic tell him otherwise. As he listens to his heart-song and finds the courage to answer its call, he embarks on an odyssey. As he continues, he will see things once invisible and do things once impossible.

Steve had lived his life in a safe zone, hoping to minimize uncertainty, smooth over imperfections, and avoid pain. He is now realizing that his safe haven was a spiritual prison. "It is in passionate leaps of faith that we propel the human spirit forward. The safety of the known leads only to boredom that stifles the experience of life. As with heroes everywhere, the course of our lives may become a beacon to others who are on their own quests."[6]

History is full of stories of common people who do extraordinary things. In surmounting anguish and pain, they listen to their souls, kindle their spirits, and give strength to others. Modern society encourages people to follow recipes or consult experts rather than find the fortitude to look inward. We buy diet books as a substitute for losing weight. We buy self-help books as an alternative to confronting our deepest fears and imperfections. We move from fad to fad without putting our heart fully into anything. We feel confused and powerless in the face of so many economic, environmental, and social challenges. Beneath our helplessness is a spiritual vacuum. It saps our faith, weakens our heart, and leaves us floundering in our flaws.

Spirit and Imperfection

Bill Irwin provides one example of what uncommon spirit can do. Excessive drinking left him blind by age twenty-eight. In his early fifties, a recovering alcoholic, he decided to hike the entire 2,167 miles of the Appalachian Trail. His seeing-eye dog was his sole companion. He faced daunting hazards: cliffs, storms, biting insects, and his own fear. Before starting, he committed himself spiritually to the journey: "I don't care how many times I fall, I can always crawl to Maine."[7] Eight months later, he became the first blind man to walk the length of the trail. How did he do it? "He never saw the trail. He just took it. He did not stick to the plan others preconceived for the life of a blind man. He sought his own course, the one his spirit needed to follow."[8]

Embedded in Bill Irwin's story are the dual messages of human imperfection and human transcendence. Irwin's youthful imperfections led to his blindness. But he embraced a maxim that offers an alternative to both shallow optimism and deep pessimism. It says, "I'm not O.K., and you're not O.K. But that's all right."[9]

Steve is struggling to accept that truth—he fears that he will discover within himself weakness, pain, or evil that can never be made right. To go forward requires him to face those fears. Only in accepting imperfection can we develop the conviction to embark on an ill-defined search for a better place. Ernest Becker, author of the Pulitzer Prize–winning book *The Denial of Death*, observed that "man is the God who shits."[10] That paradox cuts to the heart of spirituality. To deny imperfections is to deny our humanity and to become disconnected from our souls. The leader who falters, like the God who shits, is a paradox that only spirit enables us to accept and embrace.

A preacher once asked a group of children: If all the good people in the world were red and all the bad people were green, what color would you be? One girl thought for a long time, looking very serious. Then her face brightened, and she said, "Reverend, I'd be streaky."[11]

We're all streaky. Acceptance of fear and imperfection, and willingness to undertake the journey anyway, transport us to life's deepest core, "the inner value, the rapture that is associated with being alive."[12]

Gifts

CHAPTER 7

Gifts of Leadership

Late November. Gloomy sky. Chilling rain. As he trudged up the path, he could see her watching him through the window. His pace was brisk. His face told another story. Frustration. Gloom. Something unfinished.

After brief pleasantries, she got to the point. You're discouraged?

Not exactly. Ups and downs. Sometimes I'm soaring. Like a great adventure. Mistakes don't drag me down so much. You were right. Prayer helps.

You're finding heartsongs.

Particularly from Gwen.

Tell me about her.

Like you, she's a gift. You've both given me hope. I've asked Gwen to marry me.

Has she agreed?

Not yet. She's more patient than I am. Better at taking a long view.

You need someone like that.

She's got me going to church. On alternate Sundays. I'd been away too long. I'd forgotten the power. The prayers. The music. The liturgy. The feeling of community.

What about the other Sundays?

We take walks around the lake. We talk. We listen to the wind in the trees. Lunch in the same meadow each time. If you look, you find reverence in nature.

She nodded. Emily Dickinson wrote that some kept the Sabbath at church but she kept it at home, with a bobolink for a chorister and an orchard for a dome.

I should read Dickinson, he replied. Might impress Gwen. She loves female poets.

He scanned the room. Suddenly it hit him.

No photos, he said.

What?

No photos. First time I came, I felt something was missing. Beautiful art.
But no friends. No family. No
people.

He thought he saw
something different in
her eyes. Turmoil?
Sadness? Then it was
gone.

The art is enough,
she said.

Was she telling the
truth? Hiding some-
thing? Was he being
too intrusive? Avoiding
his own struggles?

She moved on, ignoring his unstated
question. You were saying mistakes don't bother you as much.

She was changing the subject. But why? He decided to let
it go.

Not as much. I'm clearer about what's important. But it's hard
to express.

Why?

When I mention spirit, other people look at me like I'm an alien.

Everyone?

Not Gwen. She understands. So do some friends. No one at work.

What happens there?

I'm the boss. They're careful. I can feel it. See it in their eyes. I've been trying to drum up support for a weekly "spirit breakfast." Right now, I'm not sure anyone would come.

You're trying to lead, but no one's following.

Like a band leader who turned left at a fork. The rest of the band turned right.

Steve, you're discovering one of life's most precious gifts. You lead with soul by giving it to others.

I know how to give direction—but not spirit.

What if I had directed you to seek your soul?

He paused. I'd have left. I wanted to anyway. Maybe it's the same with people in my organization. Sharing spirit sounds good. But how?

With gifts.

Gifts?

You said Gwen is a gift.

Right—but I'm not about to offer Gwen to my co-workers.

She laughed. Of course not. I'm talking about what Gwen has added to your life.

Hope. Love.

Maria nodded. Look at any of the great spiritual traditions. You find two moral precepts at the core. Compassion and justice. Are they at the heart of your business?

I doubt it.

You make them so through your gifts.

What kind of gifts?

Ultimately you have to discover your own gifts.

Have you found yours?

I've found four so far. I see them emerging from two basic dualities: yin and yang, matter and spirit.

He was puzzled. Dualities?

Opposites that make each other possible.

What was she talking about? Like without pain there is no joy? he asked.

That's it. Opposites in harmony. The four gifts provide balance.

My organization could use some balance.

From yin, the female principle, caring and compassion—the gift of love. From yang, the male principle, initiative and influence—the gift of power. From matter, the pragmatic world, accomplishment and craftsmanship—the gift of authorship.

And the fourth?

Later. When you're ready.

He felt a surge of anger. Come on! Was he a child? He didn't need to be spoon-fed.

She sensed his anger. Impatience only slows your journey.

She's been right before, he told himself. Tell me about authorship.

It's the feeling of putting your own signature on your work. It's the sheer joy of creating something of lasting value. The reward of adding something special to our world.

I've been working on that with our World-Class Quality program. Getting our people focused on excellence. Producing something they can be proud of.

Are you happy with the results?

Not really. The harder I push, the more they seem to push back.

You see the paradox?

Maybe I should, he said, but no.

You hope they will become what they are not. You're trying to get them to embrace something you don't think they want.

I'm trying to motivate them to do their best. Isn't that leadership?

Do you motivate a rosebush to blossom? Impel your children to grow? When you try to push from the outside instead of encouraging what's inside, you get in the way.

He felt the blood rise to his face. His throat tightened. His voice rose. Didn't you just say to give people authorship? That's exactly what I'm trying to do! How else am I supposed to motivate them to set higher standards?

Why do Zen masters teach that if you meet the Buddha on the road, kill him?

You've asked that question before.

Yes.

You think I didn't get it the first time?

Yes.

What was she trying to tell him? He looked down at the floor. He struggled to find a connection. Finally it came. Answers aren't outside. They're inside. Same for motives. I keep asking you when I should be asking myself.

He glanced out the window. The weather is lousy, he said. Still, a good time for a walk.

He started down the steps. Still raining. Cold. Windy. Should he turn around? No, he'd feel foolish. And he wanted time to himself. He closed his raincoat and plunged forward.

CHAPTER 8

Authorship

He cut the walk short. Too cold.

She handed him a drink. Here. Something to take the chill off.

The fourth gift—coffee, he replied.

She laughed. He sipped the dark brew. No cranes. Just a simple beige mug.

You were right.

About what?

Shipping my question back to me. I wanted you to do my work. You wouldn't. I had to paint my own canvas.

How did it turn out?

I realized I was doing to you what people at work do to me.

What's that?

Upward delegation. Dumping stuff in my lap.

Why do they do it?

Collusion. I love being the guy who solves the tough problems. They know I love it and give me what I want.

It's a great way to stay busy.

Swamped. With everyone else's work. They're off the hook. Protected from mistakes. And from learning. Meanwhile, I never have time for the big picture.

It's the leader's curse.

What curse?

Rugged individualism. Think of all those movie heroes. John Wayne. Clint Eastwood. Spiderman, Iron Man, and all the other superheroes. The leader saves the day while the townspeople cower in the background. It's a message we've all heard many times: If you have a problem, hope for a hero to rescue you.

But then blame the hero if things don't work out, he replied. If things go bad, it's not our fault. It's the leader's job to solve our problems.

It's sometimes different in China and Japan, she said. There, it's the group's job to solve the leader's problems.

I was thinking about BP's oil spill on my walk. The CEO got out front, promised more than he could deliver, and got

hammered. So
he was pushed
off-stage, and
they put more
emphasis
on the
people
closer
to the
action.

That
reminds me
of a story I read about two oil company executives. Both
had the same problem—a fire in a refinery. One executive
got a call at home. Rushed in. Met with his people. Got
reports from the scene. Gave orders. A frantic morning of
firefighting.

Sounds like me, he replied.

The other executive arrived in his office. Checked the morning
papers. Handled his e-mail. Thought about strategy in the
Middle East. Learned about the fire after it was under control.
Subordinates explained how they had handled it. He congratu-
lated them.

That second guy must have a better handle than I do on giving authorship. And he probably enjoys life more. I've always thought I was good at delegating. Clear about expectations. Good follow-up. But the buck still stops with me.

You're accountable in the end. But that doesn't mean your people can't feel a sense of authorship. Why don't they?

They're always looking over their shoulders. Trying to figure out what I want. Then I complain that they don't take responsibility. Vicious cycle.

Where no one wins.

If they succeed, I take credit. If they fail, I blame them. I can see now that the motivation program I put in was crazy. Trying to persuade them of what they probably wanted to do anyway— if I'd just get out of the way.

A classic pattern. You're the parent and they're the kids. You shield them from responsibility. They look to you for direction and security.

They know I have the final say. Why give me their best? They know I'll change it anyway.

You got a lot done on a short walk. She was smiling.

More than you think. I jumped ahead. Started to think about the gift of love.

How far did you get?

Not very. Stayed close to home. I started with Gwen. I love her. I know that. I wish I could express it better. I need to understand love as a gift.

What's happening with you and Gwen?

Good things. But hard to talk about. Why was she asking? She must have a reason. She always did.

I'm glad. Keep giving. You'll learn with practice.

And if I meet the Buddha?

Love him. You're making headway, she laughed. You may not even need me much longer. She walked him to the door.

He said good-bye. He wanted to say more. Why did she say he might not need her? Was she pushing him away?

CHAPTER 9

Love

It was February. Freezing. A driving rain beat against his windshield. The forecast promised snow in the mountains. He liked driving in snow. It softened things. Nothing to interrupt his solitude. A chance to think.

He thought about love. What made that word so powerful? He could talk about love with Gwen. Sometimes with his children. Never at work. Who talks about love in a corporation? You talk about it at weddings. Six months until the wedding. Gwen had finally said yes. Maybe the only love he felt sure about.

Two months until his trip to Singapore. A new acquisition there. Great company. A merger is a little like a wedding, he thought. Two different companies. We can learn from them if we don't smother them. That's the danger: we own you, so do it our way.

That's the connection. Same problem with Gwen. They had their biggest fights when he tried to make her more like him. Yet he loved her because she wasn't like him. Loving her meant treasuring who she is. The same with Singapore. It's got to be mutual.

Whiteout. Snow so heavy he couldn't see past the wipers. He pulled off the road. Turned off the ignition. Silence. He loved nights like this. But the gift of love is something deeper. More spiritual. He smiled at the thought of spirit. It wouldn't have occurred to him before he met Maria.

He heard snowplows. Droning. Clanking. As they passed, he pulled in behind.

Well after midnight, he arrived at her home. The snow had stopped. The sky was clearing quickly. He saw a light in her study. She was waiting. He had hoped she would be.

He paused to look at the night sky. Dark patches of clouds giving way to stars. The moon almost full. In the past on nights like this, the sky spoke of cosmic comedy. Tonight it spoke of love. He arrived at Maria's with a feeling of contentment.

You must be exhausted, she called from the front porch.

He was surprised. A departure from the routine. He wouldn't have to wait for her to come to the door.

Physically, yes, he called back. Spiritually, never better.

He came in. A mug of coffee was waiting.

I was starting to worry, she said.

No need. I've been driving in snow a long time. Had to stop once. Almost a total whiteout. Couldn't see a thing.

What did you do?

Pulled off. Watched the snow. Thought about love.

What happened?

A team of snowplows came along. I followed them.

I was asking about love.

I know. He looked at her. Actually, I was thinking that you've given me love since the first time we met.

He wasn't prepared for her reaction. She glanced away momentarily, but said nothing.

He continued. I didn't understand love. I thought it was just attrac-

tion and

desire.

Like a

business deal:

you invest in

the hope of a big

return. That's

not it.

She stood up. Let's talk more tomorrow. Even if you're not tired, I am. If you're hungry, try your luck in the refrigerator. How about we meet at eight?

He nodded.

We'll take a walk before breakfast, she added. It should be beautiful. She turned away.

See you in the morning, he responded.

He was puzzled. When he mentioned love, she seemed to pull back. He poured more coffee. He wandered around the house. All this art. No photos of people. *She's always intense—but always composed. What's behind her mask? Is she hiding something? Is that why she lives up here alone?*

By morning, the sunlight dazzled in the new snow. Maria was her usual self. Warm. Confident. Inscrutable. He wanted to ask about last night. He decided to start on safer ground.

How do I give love in my organization? he asked as they walked along.

She smiled. He watched her breath form a translucent cloud in the icy air. Jesus washed the feet of his disciples shortly before his death. He told them to follow his example.

How do you do that in a business?

I remember in Tokyo. Some Japanese executives spend time every week cleaning toilets. It's their gift of love.

I'd try it, but people are already looking at me a little funny.

She smiled. How do people know you care?

Maybe they don't. Particularly now. We had to lay people off last month.

How did you do it?

We did everything. Gave them plenty of notice. Supervisors met with everyone who was affected. We paid for counseling. Hired an outplacement service.

Did you talk to them yourself? she asked.

No. They're three or four levels down. I don't know most of them.

Aren't you their leader?

He paused and scanned the snow-covered landscape. You see the branches sinking under the weight of the snow? he asked.

Yes.

That's how I feel at work. Drooping under the burden. Like I've given all I can. There's not enough to go around.

Maybe you're burdened because you haven't given enough.

Not as much as the Japanese executives. By that standard, I haven't done enough to show people I care.

Do they care about you? she asked.

Never really thought about it. Caring about the boss isn't in the job description.

Do you think love is a one-way street? Why didn't you talk to the people who were laid off? Look them in the eye. Give them comfort. Show them you understood.

I was busy, he protested halfheartedly. I didn't want to undermine the chain of command.

Excuses, she said dismissively.

OK. Maybe I was afraid to face them. So I let someone else do it.

If you show people you don't care, they'll return the favor. Show them you care about them, they might surprise you.

An old message. When you give love, you get it back. But I'm not sure I believe it.

A lot of people don't. They usually don't know what they're missing. The costs are subtle.

Such as?

Disconnection. Wondering why you can't get through to people.

Like me when I first came to see you.

Exactly. But when people know someone really cares, you can see it. In their faces. And in their actions. Love really does keep on giving.

The opening he was looking for. Then why, he asked, did you reject my gift last night?

I wasn't ready.

Was I getting too close?

No, too fast.

Timing. An old lesson. Always in a hurry. He'd tried to rush her. Pin her down. She wasn't rejecting his offer. But she wouldn't be caught up in his urgency. He had more to learn.

His thoughts drifted back to his organization. With the people we laid off, I missed the moment. But I can still do something with the people who stayed. I need to get out to Topeka. Singapore too. I'm learning how to give authorship. But I'm not sure where to begin with love.

Remember that everyone's different. A big part of love is caring enough to find out what really matters to others.

I haven't been doing that enough.

What's holding you back?

Fear, mostly.

Of what?

Of getting too close. Of opening my heart to people around me. If they know me too well, will they lose respect?

How could you find out?

I'm not ready for the office toilets. But I'll find a way.

CHAPTER 10

Power

A dazzling summer day. More than a year since they first met. Flowers in full bloom lining the way to her door. He laughed as he remembered his first visit. The fear and confusion he'd brought with him. Nothing like the joy he felt at seeing her again.

How was Singapore? she asked.

Tough. Even worse than I expected. But it came out all right.

What happened?

I tried to show them I cared. My gift of love.

Were they looking for that?

No. Not at first. Lots of polite smiles. But you could feel the chill. They had a reception. I gave a little speech. I talked about caring. It flopped.

How could you tell?

Arms crossed, blank faces.

Then what happened?

I went out on the factory floor. One of the workers, a young guy with a big, earnest smile, asked me to take a turn on his machine. I didn't have much choice. Big crowd circled around. I felt like a lamb cornered by hungry wolves. I was fumbling all over the place. I probably turned out 100 percent scrap. People thought it was hilarious.

And they loved you for it?

Just being out on the floor was the big thing. Talking to people. Saying hello. Answering questions. I think I passed a test. On the way out, I met this woman. Maybe fifty years old, Chinese, tough looking. Came up and threw her arms around me. Told me everyone figured all I cared about was money. "Now," she says, "we have a friend in America."

How did you feel?

When a factory worker in Singapore gives you a hug, that's pretty amazing.

Love only works when people feel it and believe it. She smiled. Groups create testing grounds. They're like sacred spaces, but most of the time we don't even know they're there. When you're in one and you give from your heart, people know it's real.

Not in Topeka.

What happened there?

Timing was bad. Six months after the layoffs. I knew it would be tough. But I worked in Topeka my first job out of college. I thought we were still family.

A risky assumption.

I found that out. Ran into this big guy, looks like he could have been a linebacker in the NFL. Runs a forklift. Abrasive as hell. Anyway, as soon as I get there, he's in my face, screaming. I'd fired his friends. He tells me I'm a phony, pretending we're one big happy family. Like all those other overpaid big shots.

That must have stung.

Worse than that tree limb. Torture. You know how it feels, hanging out there?

I've been there. I still have the scars.

It got worse. I felt like I'd walked into a place where I wasn't wanted and people hated me. Scowls. Subtle sarcasm. They knew how to twist the knife. End of the day, I was battered. Sat in the hotel room, nursing a glass of wine. Feeling sorry for myself. Wondering where I could hide. Just wanting out of there.

That's when you called me, isn't it? You woke me up.

It wasn't that late. I thought you'd be awake.

I wasn't feeling well that evening. I was tired.

I'll call earlier next time. Are you OK?

There's a lot of stuff going around this summer.

You helped me see that I'd brought the wrong gift. Bad timing again. I was offering love. They were saying bullshit, why'd you fire our friends? They weren't looking for caring. Not from me anyway. They wanted power.

She laughed. You dug yourself in pretty deep. Did you ever get out?

Not before I ate a lot of dirt. Next day we had this meeting. Old conference room in the plant. Cramped, bare walls, fluorescents, Formica table, plastic chairs. Martha Mendez, the union head, and her executive committee on one side of the table. Me and the plant manager on the other. They're mad. I'm cornered. Mendez lays it all out. Rakes me and management over the coals. I'm biting my tongue so hard it bleeds.

Have your wounds healed?

They're better. I sat there. Listened, asked questions. Told them I got the message. They felt betrayed. We'd been talking about listening, participation, empowerment for a long time. Then when something big comes along we get amnesia. "You admit you blew it?" Mendez asks.

How did you respond?

I choked on the words, but I said yes.

You were pretty far out on a limb.

Fifty feet above a rock quarry and she was revving up her chain saw. I promised two things. Next time, I said, we'll listen. And we'll work with you to make this plant successful.

Layoffs are bad for credibility. Did they believe you?

No, not at first. But a couple of weeks later I got invited back. Some workers and managers had banded together to develop some proposals. They'd done their homework. Gathered data. Called other plants. Worked through some disagreements. Finally agreed on what needed to be done. Some of it needed help from headquarters. Another test, I guess. I almost flunked.

How?

One guy in the group threw a half-baked idea in the hopper. No way we could spend that kind of money without a more careful look. I almost told him flat out it was a dumb idea. I bit my tongue and thought hard. Then I asked him to lead a group to study it further. He was proud.

Sounds like a good move. Caving in doesn't empower people. You set a good example. You went to the plant. You listened. You were open. You didn't lean on your authority as their boss.

Some of their ideas were terrific. Easy to say yes to. That night, Mendez invited me to her house for barbecue. The whole union executive committee was there. Best team-building session I ever saw.

What did you learn?

You can give power away and wind up with more. You remember the old gasoline ad? I always thought power was like the tiger in the tank. You don't want to let the tiger out, you just let people hear him roar.

Hoard power, dampen spirit.

That's what I learned in Topeka.

CHAPTER 11

Significance

The drive up the mountain seemed longer. He didn't mind. He was enjoying the fall colors. When he finally arrived, he walked up the familiar path.

He was surprised, troubled when she opened the door. The gray in her hair and lines in her face had always been there. But not the first thing you noticed. Was she tired? Sick? Her face gave no other clue. Her eyes and her smile were as mysterious as ever.

She motioned him in. There's hot coffee.

He thanked her. Notice the headline this morning? Another CEO fired over a sex scandal.

She nodded.

How can you have it all and still have nothing? he asked.

Do you remember yourself when we first met?

Was she baiting another hook? She kept him alert, anyway. Forced him to think.

You're right. The higher I climbed, the less I understood why or what it meant.

You felt insignificant.

Meaning what?

You were hollow at the core. No soul, no spirit, nothing.

How about some credit for progress?

Do you want to talk about the past or the future?

Maria, you are the most demanding, infuriating—

She interrupted and gestured toward the door. It caught him by surprise. You called this meeting. You can leave whenever you want.

Leave! I just drove three hours to get here. He paused and laughed at himself. Not even an E for effort?

She laughed too. She must have known how he would react. How's your spirit? she asked. Her tone was gentler.

I remember the first time you asked. I figured you weren't playing with a full deck. It didn't make any sense. Now it makes a lot.

You've learned. But something is on your mind.

The fourth gift. You never told me what it was.

No need. You already know.

And?

What were we just talking about?

About how infuriating you are.

Before that.

The CEO who harassed an employee. Having it all and still having nothing. Feeling insignificant.

Why not start there? she asked.

I did feel insignificant. Not now. Things make more sense. He paused, grasping for the right word. Significance! That's what the fourth gift is about. Why hadn't he seen that before? Then it hit him. That's what you've given me.

Now you can give it to others.

How?

You know about authorship. It's your organization. What comes to mind?

Times when I've felt significant. Maybe what works for me will apply to my organization.

Keep going.

Like my visit to Singapore. It was like being present at a birth. Coming together to generate something new. The power of shared emotion. Creating a common spirit that touched everyone.

How did it happen?

Maybe magic. Maybe love. I'm not sure. We prepared—a lot. Somehow, everyone knew the script, even though it wasn't written down. It felt very spontaneous.

That's how good rituals feel.

Bad ones can backfire, though. My lesson in Topeka began as a disaster. I thought I was Santa Claus bringing gifts. They thought I was Scrooge blowing away their friends.

What did you learn from that?

You can't impose significance. People have to create it together.

Exactly. Significance comes from doing something worth doing, making a difference in the world.

My work makes a difference. But you helped me see why it matters.

You can do the same with your people.

How?

Help people see the difference they make. Paint a picture or tell a story that helps them see how their work contributes to something bigger. It can be as simple as putting production workers in touch with customers or people in the community so they can see the impact of their work.

It seems so obvious. But it's not something I've thought much about.

So start. If you look, you'll find lots of ways to do it. Then you confirm and deepen it with celebrations.

Celebrations?

Memorable events for special occasions. Holiday parties. Summer picnics. Annual sales meetings. Quarterly off-site retreats. Rituals and ceremonies can connect people to one another and to a deeper, spiritual world—the corporate soul.

He looked skeptical. We have a holiday party every December. Plenty of spirits. But not much soul.

Then you're missing an opportunity. When done well, celebrations weave hearts and souls into a shared destiny. People summon spirit by coming together to mark beginnings and endings, triumphs and tragedies, births and deaths.

Add another item to my list of things we don't do enough in my business.

Most don't. So you lose the spiritual glue that holds people together. Think about religion. What are the ties there that bond people to one another?

He thought for a while. You know the Emerald Buddha? he finally asked.

In Bangkok. I remember it vividly.

The faithful come to pray every day. The King of Thailand visits three times a year to change the Buddha's clothes. Fit the costume to the season.

A place of great reverence.

Like the Cathedral of Notre-Dame in Paris. I remember standing there in awe. The architecture, candles, statues, paintings of the saints, figures of Mary and Jesus. A group of visiting nuns sang a hymn a cappella. Spontaneously. It took my breath away. Two feelings at once. I was going deeply into my own soul and at the same time I was soaring, joining with others.

That's the power of spirit. It fuses place, music, art, souls. It gives the everyday world rapture and mystery.

Another memory. Some friends invited me to their son's bris. As the ceremony began, the father sat holding his son. His father stood behind him. Afterward I saw tears welling up in the grandfather's eyes. He told me that standing behind his son and grandson, he felt the presence of his own father and grandfather. The eternal human chain. Right there in that moment. I felt cheated. No one did much to mark special moments in my life. We went through the motions, but the spirit wasn't there.

Do you want your employees to feel the way you did as a boy?

No, I just never made the connection before. We don't celebrate enough. We're cheating ourselves.

Do you tell stories?

What kind of stories?

Take this conversation. I asked you about spiritual bonds. You told stories. The Emerald Buddha. Your visit to Notre-Dame. Memories of a bris.

A lightbulb flashed.

When you first talked to me about spirit and heart, I had no idea what you were talking about. You told stories. Parables. The stream that wanted to cross the desert. The young man too focused on his path to see anything else.

Stories take us to the world of spirit.

That's hard to buy if you grew up worshiping at the altar of facts and logic.

We're all flooded with facts and detail. More than we can handle. The information tide keeps rising, and the world seems more out of control. Check the news on TV or the Web. What do you find?

He frowned. Murders. Political gridlock. Violence somewhere halfway round the world. It's depressing.

Then you visit Notre-Dame, she said softly. Or you attend a bris. You enter another world and touch spirit.

Fall flowers were everywhere as he walked to his car. Maybe it's there in the flowers, he thought. He remembered a Zen story. The Buddha preached a sermon by lifting up a flower. *The meaning in the flowers is that they're there,* he thought. *And my meaning is that I'm here. I'm alive.*

On the drive home he was flooded with questions about how to infuse his organization with significance. He laughed. He remembered how often the possessive pronoun *my* had got him in trouble in the past. For people to feel significant, he knew the organization had to be *ours,* not *mine.*

CHAPTER 12

Corporate Community

A soggy day in March. Rutted dirt road. When would this detour end? Was he on the wrong road? Would the rain ever stop? Questions tumbled through his mind. Why did little irritants still annoy him so much? Like the erosion of customer survey data. Why hadn't he seen it coming? Again. Above all, how was Maria?

It was dark when he finally reached her place. She was reading with music in the background. Mozart? Mahler? He wasn't sure. She seemed stronger. A big relief.

You got a late start?

No, a flood washed out part of the road. Felt like I was on a detour to nowhere. Trapped in a river of mud.

Did you consider your plight a gift?

Not at first. He smiled. But it got me thinking about bogs. And bumps in the road. At work. In life.

Hard roads are better teachers. They take us to new places.

Since I met you, I've had more than my share of hard roads.

You were finding easier ones before?

I wasn't finding any before. I was off in a ditch somewhere. He smiled. I'm not blaming you. It's not your fault I haven't reached paradise yet.

You won't in this life.

I know. Maybe the next one.

But you can find peace.

Have you?

More than once.

I'm not there yet.

You will be. She smiled. I'm praying for us both.

Was she dropping a hint? She went on before he could ask.

So, what's bogging you down?

I'm seeing fragments here and there. But how to put them together? For a long time, it was all about me. You helped me get from me to us. From taking to giving. I'm starting to see where I need to go, but I'm not sure how to get there.

Where is there?

Some of my people are telling me we're not thinking big enough, we're too insular.

How so?

We're too caught up in our own world. Not thinking far enough beyond our company. How we relate to customers. Suppliers. Communities we're part of. Everyone we touch.

Spirit flows across boundaries.

I know. Same for gifts. So we need to give outside as well as inside. But how do we do that? Will the same gifts work?

Why not?

Not sure. You once told me I wasn't giving enough. That may still be true. But going beyond the organization seems overwhelming.

Try breaking it down to one external group at a time. How about customers?

We're getting troubling data about customer satisfaction.

What are they saying?

We're too slow. We don't listen. If you call customer service, you get a series of voice mail prompts, then get bounced from one representative to another. Finally you reach someone who doesn't understand your problem and can't do anything about it.

What does that tell you about the gifts customers are asking for?

He thought for a minute. Well, authorship, for one. How do we make it easier for them to put their mark on the product? Power for another. They want to feel that they can get our attention and action. Particularly when they have a problem. Tech support that actually does what it is supposed to. We've relied too much on the idea that if it sells, it's what customers want.

Because if it's not, they can buy from someone else?

And they probably will if we don't make it easier for them to get what they're looking for. We talk about being close to the customer. They're telling us we're not close enough.

How much time do you spend with customers?

Not enough. I read all the reports. Meet with big accounts. I need to do more.

It costs you if you don't.

Tell me something I don't know.

You can't depend on me forever. I cued up the question. You take it from there.

Fair enough. First, if I don't spend time with customers, I won't know how we're doing.

And?

And I'm sending a message to my people. If it's not important to me, maybe it's not that crucial to them either.

Bravo! Her voice was soft, but he still felt her enthusiasm. Now, what else could you do?

We need to give our customer service people more clout, so they can solve problems without going up the hierarchy.

Why haven't you done it already?

Fear, probably.

Of what?

Losing control of costs—or people.

You don't trust your people?

Ouch! His tone was more playful than annoyed.

The question stings?

Hits too close. I spent a lot of my life not trusting people. Probably cost me my first marriage. Never again. We want our customers to feel they'd rather do business with us than our competitors. We have to trust our people so they can better serve our customers.

How about love?

I love everyone who buys our product.

Do they know that?

They don't. They're telling us they're not feeling the love.

Do your people feel it?

More and more.

The more they feel it, the better they can share it.

If they know that's what we expect. They're focused on following the rules and keeping costs down. That's not good enough. We don't have good metrics for what's most important. Are they giving customers what they want?

Isn't that what they'd like to do anyway?

Probably.

So you've been rewarding A while hoping for B?

A is easy to measure. B is harder. But if we can figure out how to tackle B, we'll be well ahead of our competitors. Their service is no better than ours.

What about significance? Beyond how it's used, what does your product mean to your customers?

We're looking for answers. We'd like to generate more passion in our customers. Like Apple. Subaru. In-N-Out Burger. We're looking for our own secret sauce.

Who's doing the looking?

It's a shared effort. I'm hoping the more we confer significance on our people, the more they'll pass it on to our customers.

What about the larger community?

At least we've stopped being stupid.

How so?

Like the time the EPA was after us about toxic chemicals in the water. We spent more money on a PR campaign claiming it wasn't a problem than it would have cost us to do the cleanup. Damaged our image, and eventually we had to pay for the cleanup anyway.

Whose idea was the PR campaign?

He paused, looking embarrassed. Mine.

What are you doing instead?

The usual stuff. Donating to good causes. Encouraging our people to volunteer in their community. We're getting better at being green.

You're getting closer to the essence.

Which is?

When giving becomes a way of life, essential to who you are. With everyone you touch.

We're feeling our way. Last month, employees at headquarters took a day to build a playground for neighborhood kids. The look on those kids' faces said it all, but the pride and stories our people brought back with them lit up the office.

Were you there?

Handling a shovel and pitching in with a group putting up a jungle gym. It was hard work. Surprised Gwen when I came home grungy and limping. But it was a great day.

So you've made progress, but you know you need to go further?

He nodded. I read somewhere that in order to be a great company, you have to be good first. I hope we're on our way. But I still wonder sometimes if being good is always good for business? If we don't make money, I'll be out of a job.

Is the job worth keeping if you're not offering as much to the world as it gives to you?

No. I guess it comes down to a question of faith. I have more work to do.

But you've come a long way.

I've started saying to people that soul is who we are, spirit is how we express it. Some of our younger people are pushing me to go further.

What are they saying?

They're asking for a company-wide conversation about how we relate to our community and the environment. We've been getting clearer about who we are internally, but we haven't put it together externally. What kind of citizen do we want to be? What gifts should we offer beyond our boundaries?

That sounds exciting.

I've been putting it off, but it's getting clearer that's where we need to go.

Another tough road.

That's OK if we're on the right course.

Community and the Cycle of Giving

Find the real world, give it endlessly away
Grow rich, fling gold to all who ask
Live at the empty heart of Paradox
I'll dance there with you, cheek to cheek.

—Rumi[1]

Leading is giving. It is an ethic, a gift of oneself to a common cause. It is easy to miss the message's depth and power. The dialogues between Steve and Maria are intended to encourage you to deepen your internal journey in search of gifts you can offer others. Without giving there can be no real leadership.

The essence of leadership is not giving tangible things or even inspirational visions. It is offering oneself and one's spirit. Material gifts are not unimportant. We need both bread and roses. Soul and spirit are not substitutes for wages and working conditions. But what we have all heard is true—the most important thing about a gift is the spirit behind it. When Steve approached gift giving as a material transaction, he failed. In offering his soul, he set in motion a reciprocal process—others gave of themselves in return. Authorship, caring, power, and significance only work when they are freely given and genuinely received. Leaders cannot give what they do not have. If they try, they only breed disappointment and cynicism. Yet when the gifts are genuine and the spirit is right, gift giving transforms an organization from a place of work to a shared way of life.

In Figure 1, we embed the four gifts in a mandala. In its root meaning, a mandala is container of essence, and the diagram

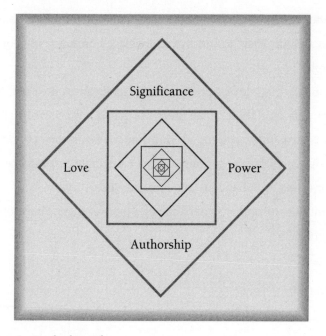

Figure 1 Leadership Gifts
Source: www.free-mandala.com

suggests that each of the gifts is distinct, but all are intercon-nected parts of a larger, spiritual whole.

The leader's quest is "a journey to find the treasure of your true self, and then [to return] home to give your gift to help transform the kingdom—and in the process your own life. The quest is replete with dangers and pitfalls, but it offers equivalent rewards: the capacity to be successful in the world, knowledge of the mysteries of the human soul, and opportunities to find your unique gifts, and to live in loving community with other people."[2]

Authorship, love, power, and significance are not the only gifts that leaders can offer. As Maria told Steve, leaders must learn for themselves the contribution that is theirs to make. Any gifts will work, so long as they contribute to fundamental ethics like compassion and justice. Fused with soul and spirit, gifts form the cornerstone of a purposeful and passionate community.

The Gift of Love

And what is it to work with love?
It is to weave the cloth with threads drawn
from your own heart,
even as if your beloved
were to wear that cloth.
It is to charge all things you fashion
with a breath of your own spirit,
Work is love made visible
And if you cannot work with love but only
with distaste, it is better that you should

leave your work and sit at the gate of the
temple and take alms of those who work with joy.

—Kahlil Gibran[3]

Asked about the secret of her leadership, Mother Teresa answered, "Small work with great love."[4] Love is the true hallmark of great leaders—love for their work and for those with whom they work. Pressures of task and the bottom line often crowd out personal needs that people bring into the workplace. There's always so much to be done. Who has time for kind words, or listening, or caring? Andrew Delios questioned whether organizations can "dare to care" and still be competitive,[5] but Jeffrey Pfeffer has argued that caring is a proven route to an improved bottom line.[6] Danny Meyer, founder of several of the most successful restaurants in the intensely competitive New York market—including Gramercy Park and Union Square—credits his success to five core values: "caring for each other, caring for guests, caring for the community, caring for suppliers, and caring for investors and profitability—in descending order of importance."[7]

When Motorola founder Paul Galvin was asked for his philosophy of business, he replied: "Five words, to love and to achieve. And the second will never happen until you do the first." To this day, the word *love* is no stranger to people who work at Motorola—or at Subaru Motors, where building cars people love to drive is a priority. The theme was extended in 2009 to an end-of-year "Share the Love" program, during which the company contributed $250 to charity for every vehicle sold. At Southwest Airlines, love is a watchword that is passed along to passengers. Southwest founder Herb Kelleher once said his company's culture was built around the principle of "caring for people in the totality of their lives," and Bo Burlingham found that the same quality was present in all of the "small giants" that he studied—entrepreneurial firms that had achieved unusual success by pursuing purposes that transcended growth or profits.[8] Unfortunately, too many organizations encourage amiable superficiality and discourage deeper forms of human contact. In most workplaces, the unwritten rules are clear: stay on task, be friendly and upbeat, and avoid anything that hints at emotion or intimacy.

Every organization is a family, whether caring or dysfunctional. Caring begins with knowing—it requires listening, understanding, and accepting. It progresses through a deepening sense of appreciation, respect, and ultimately love. Steve hesitated to embrace love because he recognized the risk of vulnerability in reaching out and opening his heart. Yet embracing that risk lets us drop our masks, meet heart to heart, and be present for one another. We experience a sense of unity and delight in those voluntary, human exchanges that mold "the soul of community."[9]

Love has probably received more attention than any other human emotion. It has many meanings. Plato called it divine madness.[10] The poet Guiraut de Bornelh saw a more tender side:

> Love is born, who its fair hope
> Goes comforting her friends.
> For as all true lovers know, love is perfect
> kindness
> Which is born—there is no doubt—from the
> heart and eyes.
> The eyes make it blossom; the heart matures it
> Love, which is the fruit of their very seed.[11]

Love is largely absent in the modern corporation. Most managers would never use the word in any context more profound than their feelings about food, films, or games. They shy away from love's deeper meanings, fearing both its power and its risks. So it was with Steve. In Topeka, he tried to minimize his risk and liability. Only by accepting anguish and vulnerability—companions of love—could he offer a gift that was both accepted and appreciated.

The Gift of Authorship

Authorship is rare in most organizations. Though it may sound like a caricature from a Dickens novel, the classic management approach is simple. Give people a job. Tell them how to do it. Look over their shoulder to make sure they're doing it right. Reward or punish them depending on their performance. It's frustrating for everyone. Workers feel overcontrolled, underinformed, and undervalued. Even when they know how to do the job better than their boss, they feel compelled to follow orders at the expense of performance. Disappointed superiors blame workers and tighten supervision. A constricting spiral undermines workers' sense of connection, ownership, and pride.

Despite efforts across corporate America to increase participation and enhance the quality of work, tens of thousands of people still see their work as just a job—they put in time, go through the motions, and collect a check. Around the world, employees have developed similar levels of cynicism. In the Soviet era, Russian workers elegantly captured the sentiment in the aphorism, "We pretend to work and they pretend to pay us."

Authorship turns the classic organizational pyramid on its side and provides space within boundaries. Leaders increase their influence and build more productive organizations.

Workers experience the satisfactions of creativity, craftsmanship, and a job well done. Authorship transcends the traditional adversarial relationship in which superiors try to increase their control while subordinates resist them at every turn. Trusting people to solve problems generates higher levels of motivation and better solutions. The leader's responsibility is to create conditions that promote authorship. Individuals need to see their work as meaningful and worthwhile, to feel personally accountable for the consequences of their efforts, and to get feedback that lets them know the results.[12]

Saturn Motors in its heyday was a tangible showcase of what the gift of authorship can accomplish. The company took GM employees and gave them a chance to make their own decisions and put their signature on a car someone eventually would drive. As one Saturn employee remarked, "Given the opportunity anyone would like to produce a perfect product. At Saturn they have given us that opportunity, that chance." Under a plant manager who had given the gift of authorship, one auto worker commented, "We make decisions now. Before, we never made no decisions. We just ran the machine and that was it!"

Google provides a contemporary example of the power of authorship. Among the many ways that Google supports the expression and development of talent is its 70/20/10 time allocation model—10 percent of an engineer's time is allocated for "innovation, creativity and freedom to think," while 20 percent is for "personal development that will ultimately benefit the company." In terms of revenue per employee, Google's staff is among the most productive on the planet.

The Gift of Power

The idea of power as a gift may seem paradoxical. Can anyone ever give power to someone else? Would they even if they could? Realists and revolutionaries have long believed that no one but a fool ever gives away power. Power, they argue, must be seized—forced unwillingly from the hands of those who clutch it. This might be true if giving power always meant becoming weaker. Yet Steve's most important lesson at the Topeka plant was that giving power could make him stronger.

Hoarding power produces a powerless organization. People stripped of power look for ways to fight back: foot-dragging, sabotage, withdrawal, or angry militancy. Violence is the poetry of powerlessness. Powerlessness fuels rebellion, coercion, even terrorism. We see tragic examples of this self-sealing spiral every day in organizations and societies around the world. Conversely, giving power liberates energy for more productive use. When people have a sense of efficacy and an ability to influence their world, they strive to be productive. They direct their energy and intelligence toward making a contribution rather than obstructing progress or destroying their enemies. Amid the wave of unrest that swept the Arab world in early 2011, there were examples in one country after another of newly empowered citizens voluntarily stepping in to clean streets, direct traffic, and distribute food until government was again able to perform its usual functions. Progressive auto companies have given employees the power to stop the assembly line when they spot something amiss. A rope with a handle is located at various places in the manufacturing process. When they see deviations from standards, employees pull the rope and stop the line. Giving clout helps produce a superior product.

The gift of power enrolls people in working toward a common cause. It also creates difficult choice points, like the one Steve faced when an employee "threw a half-baked idea into the hopper." In such circumstances, if leaders just say no and clutch power tightly, they reactivate old patterns of antagonism. If they cave in and say yes to anything, they put the organization's mission at risk. The gift Steve offered to the worker was not like a coin placed in an outstretched hand or a neatly wrapped gift placed under a tree. What Steve gave was an *opportunity* for the worker to empower himself. Like all the gifts that he and Maria discussed, the gift of power can only be given to those who want it and are ready to receive it.

Leaders cannot empower others by disempowering themselves. They need to help others find and make productive use of many sources of power—information, resources, allies, access, and autonomy.[13] The workers and managers who banded together at the Topeka plant tapped many of those sources to give their recommendations the power that made it easy for Steve to say yes.

The gift of power is closely linked to conflict. When power is hoarded and centralized, conflict is often suppressed. Eventually it emerges in coercive or explosive forms. One example is the violence in many urban neighborhoods. Feeling powerless, seeing society as an enemy, young people try to empower themselves through gangs and guns. A deeper and more destructive dynamic has arisen in the many places around the globe that have become breeding grounds for terrorism.

Recent research suggests that terrorism is most likely to emerge from a toxic stew with several key ingredients:[14]

- A perception of wounds and victimhood in the wake of long-standing discrimination or social injustice

- A repressive but illegitimate and ineffectual regime that blocks free expression and undermines the rule of law
- Rapid social and technical change that unmoors traditional beliefs and values

The wounds and victimhood provide motivational fire. Political repression blocks expression of grievance. Rapid change precipitates a sense that everything is falling apart, and there is no hope of anything positive under the existing regime. Seeing the gates of opportunity closed and no other avenues for positive action, some individuals turn to terror. In his treatise on the roots of terror, Bjørgo argues that terrorists are not crazy.[15] They are rational actors who see violence as the most promising path toward reducing inequality and redressing injustice. Their perspective gives them a way to feel empowered in a world that makes little sense, but the price is high. Instead of using their talents to create something that carries their positive signature, they add to the toll of murder and mayhem. The lesson is clear: individuals want to express themselves and to make a difference. Those impulses often get distorted when an organization or a society fails to provide outlets for their expression.

People who feel genuinely powerful will find productive options. But in the messy time that follows a highly centralized system loosening up, the initial outcomes are often surprising and disturbing. Previously hidden conflicts leap to the surface. Interest groups battle for control and scarce resources. This happened all over Eastern Europe after the collapse of Soviet Communism. It happened in Iraq after Saddam Hussein's regime was toppled, and across the Arab world in early 2011. Effective leadership gives power without undermining the system's integrity. At its best, the gift of power makes it possible to confront conflict without warfare and violence. Scott Peck has observed that community is "a place where conflict can be resolved without physical or emotional bloodshed and with wisdom as well as grace."[16]

Authorship and power are related, so the two are easily confused. Space and freedom are at issue in both. Yet there is an important difference. Authorship requires autonomy. Power is the ability to influence others. Artists, authors, scientists, and skilled craftspeople can experience high levels of authorship, even when they work largely by themselves. Power, in contrast, is meaningful only in relationship to others. It is the capacity to influence and get things to happen on a broader scale. Authorship without power is isolating and splintering. Power without authorship can be dysfunctional and oppressive. Each of these two gifts is incomplete. Together, their impact on organizational spirit is extraordinary, a lesson taken to heart by pioneering companies from camping (Recreational Equipment Inc.) to cartoons (Dreamworks), fibers (W. L. Gore) to finance (Edward Jones), or software (Google and SAS) to supermarkets (Wegmans and Whole Foods).

The Gift of Significance

Howard Schultz built Starbucks as a coffee company with a heart. The response was overwhelming and Starbucks' outlets mushroomed across America and the world. As years passed, however, Schultz withdrew from his role as CEO, growth took its toll, and outlets begin to lose their neighborhood coffee shop aura.

This prompted Schultz to return as CEO in 2008. The first thing he felt he needed to do was to "stand up in front of the entire company and admit, almost as a confession, that the leadership of the company had failed the 180,000 Starbucks people and their families, and even though I wasn't the CEO, I was around as chairman, and I smelled it. I wasn't engaged. But I'm responsible." That made it possible to work on preserving and enhancing "the only asset we've ever had as a company—our values, our culture and guiding principles, and a reservoir of trust with our people." He sent out a memo emphasizing that the company had lost its way: "Starbucks no longer has the soul of the past. It is now a chain of stores vs. the warm feeling of a neighborhood store." He took 10,000 store managers to a meeting in New Orleans where they began with a day of community service because Schultz was convinced it would be a powerful way to remind leaders of the real significance of what they did. He saw the New Orleans meeting as vital in getting Starbucks back on track.[17] Like most businesses, Starbucks struggled in the recession of 2008 and 2009, but came back with record earnings by 2010. A company's sense of significance is easy to lose, but can be rebuilt by sensitive and persistent leadership. No one can take your soul from you. You have to give it away or lose it. But you can always find it again or take it back.

There are also potential shadows to tight-knit normative communities. History gives many examples of supposedly liberating societies that turned out to be oppressive, intolerant, or unjust. Every major religion has seen instances of leaders who used spiritual authority for selfish or destructive ends. Parallel risks exist in any group or organization. Community, like love, carries risks of dependence, exploitation, and loss. But it makes no more sense to reject the ideal of community than to shun intimacy. We need to approach both with a combination of hope and wisdom.

Among the most vital building blocks of community are the many forms of expressive and symbolic experience: rituals, ceremonies, icons, music, and stories. Humans have always created and used symbols as a foundation for meaning and significance. Organizations without a rich symbolic life become empty and sterile—places where going to work is about as satisfying as going to a restaurant and eating the menu. What is missed is the joy of sharing something meaningful with others. The magic of special occasions is vital in building significance into collective life. Moments of ecstasy or grief are parentheses that mark life's major passages. Without ritual and ceremony, transitions remain incomplete, a clutter of comings and goings. "Life becomes an endless set of Wednesdays."[18] When ritual and ceremony are authentic and attuned, they fire the imagination, evoke insight, and touch the heart. Ceremony weaves past, present, and future into life's ongoing tapestry. Ritual helps us face and comprehend life's everyday shocks, triumphs, and mysteries. Both help us experience the unseen webs of significance that tie a community together. When inauthentic, such occasions become meaningless, repetitious, and alienating. They waste our time, disconnect us from work, and splinter us from one another. "Community must become more than just gathering the troops, telling the stories, and remembering things past.

Community must also be rooted in values that do not fail, values that go beyond the self-aggrandizement of human leaders."[19]

Ceremony and ritual may seem exotic and far removed from the ordinary requirements of life. There are grand ceremonies for special occasions—product launches, retirements, award extravaganzas, and annual picnics. There are simple rituals—coffee breaks, softball teams, and the after-hours cocktail or beer—that infuse meaning, passion, and purpose into daily routine. Both speak to the soul:

> A piece of clothing [like a company T-shirt or baseball cap] may be useful, but it may also have special meaning to a theme of the soul. It is worth going to a little trouble to make a dinner a ritual by attending to the symbolic suggestiveness of the food and the way it is presented and eaten. Without this added dimension, which requires some thought, it may seem that life goes on smoothly, but slowly soul is weakened and can make its presence known only in symptoms.[20]

Like ritual and ceremony, narrative is a vessel for soul and spirit. It was difficult for Steve or Maria to talk about significance without the stories that they shared. Stories transport us to the magical realm of spirit.

Like night dreams, stories often use symbolic language, thus bypassing the ego and persona and traveling straight to the spirit and soul, who listen for the ancient and universal instructions embedded there. Because of this process, stories can teach, correct errors, lighten the heart and the darkness, provide psychic shelter, assist transformation, and heal wounds. . . . The tales people tell one another weave a strong fabric that can warm the coldest emotional or spiritual nights. So the stories that rise up out of the group become, over time, both extremely personal and quite eternal, for they take on a life of their own when told over and over again.[21]

In successful organizations, people's sense of significance is rooted in shared stories, passed from person to person and generation to generation. They tell about people and events, triumphs and tragedies. They transcend time and place. Steve is beginning to understand stories as the symbolic narrative that holds a group together:

Some say that community is based on blood ties, sometimes dictated by choice, sometimes by necessity. And while this is quite true, the immeasurably stronger gravitational field that holds a group together are their stories . . . the common and simple ones they share with one another.[22]

In writing this book, we deliberately chose the word *significance* for its dual connotations of meaning and importance. The gift of significance lets people find meaning in work, faith in themselves, confidence in the value of their lives, and hope for the future. Work becomes more joy than drudgery, an opportunity to make a difference as well as a living. Reason and technology often divert our attention from the everyday, existential pillars that support our sense of meaning and purpose. If we lose our gift of fantasy and festival, we lose one of life's most precious gifts. Steve is realizing all this for himself. He is beginning to see that the gifts of love, authorship, power, and significance intertwine to form the tapestry of his company's soul and spirit.

Giving to the Community

Christine Arena calls them "high purpose companies"—businesses that consider profits a means to the more important end of making a durable contribution to society. They use their economic leverage to "build social and economic value, to raise hope, and extinguish despair."[23] In their classic exploration of corporate citizenship, *Beyond Good Company,* Googins, Mirvis, and Rochlin note that a dramatic shift is under way in how people in and out of business think about the relationship between corporations and society. Some business leaders still adhere to the minimalist view expressed by one CEO who said, "My view of corporate responsibility is that death and jail scare me, but if no one dies and I stay out of jail, it's OK." A number of developments are pushing business leaders toward more holistic perspectives. One is the spate of scandals in which corporate greed and ethical lapses have damaged the economy, the environment, and society, spawning greater distrust of business and more government intervention. A second factor is the growing consensus that our globe is on a path to environmental crises such as global warming and resource depletion. A multi-year study from 2001 to 2005 found that the public is demanding more but seeing less in terms of corporations' meeting their responsibilities to society.[24]

As a result, the idea of "corporate citizenship" is growing in popularity, despite disagreement about what it means. Some business leaders see it as "employee volunteering and charity,"[25] but it is much more than that. Googins and his colleagues argue for a broader view because "business has its biggest impact on society through (1) its own operations and (2) its interactions with myriad suppliers, distributors and partners through the entire value chain to end users."[26] A comprehensive view of corporate citizenship should encompass "the harms and benefits of a company's commercial activities on society."[27] This leads to two basic criteria:

> *Minimize harm:* Take account of and minimize the negative impact of a firm's footprint in society. The main injunction is "do no harm."
>
> *Maximize benefit:* Create *shared value* in the form of economic wealth *and* social welfare, including reduction of poverty, improvement of health and well-being, development of people, and care of the natural environment. Here the message is "do good."[28]

As he deepens his understanding of what it means to lead with soul, Steve is seeing that an ethic of giving has to apply outside as well as inside. He needs to go beyond his own organization to ask what his business can give to society and the environment. As Maria tells him, spirit wants to flow across boundaries. Steve will need to learn from the examples of progressive companies like General Electric, Nike, Starbucks, and Unilever, which have come to appreciate the need for a comprehensive, long-term approach to citizenship that is integrated into their business strategy and rooted in a sense of who they are and what they value. Steve recognizes that this will be difficult and risky. In talking to Maria, he expresses a concern of many business leaders: will too much focus on corporate responsibility hurt the bottom line and ultimately his career? Overcoming such fears will take time, learning, experimentation, and leadership.

Sharing

CHAPTER 13

Summoning the Magic of Stories

He wanted to deny it. He no longer could. She was ill. Canceled meetings. Delays in returning calls. Weariness in her voice when she finally did. He was praying with new urgency. Prayer might not improve her health, but it was his heartsong. His way of keeping faith. He'd learned it from her.

His eyes rebelled against the harsh sunlight. Heat shimmered from the road ahead. Even with the air-conditioning on full blast, it still felt oppressive. *It'll be better in the mountains*, he thought. A flood of memories was a welcome distraction. He recalled his first trip up this road. How miserable he felt then. She'd helped him find a way out of his private hell. Now he understood that spirit is the real life flow. In his life. In his work. Did she know how much she had given? He hoped so.

A note on her door directed him to the back porch. She was napping there. He'd never seen her asleep. He missed seeing her eyes. Intense. Beacons on his journey. Reflections of soul.

He sat and waited. Not for long. She seemed to sense his presence. She smiled broadly when she saw him. Her usual vitality seemed to return.

Steve, I'm glad you're here. There's lemonade in the refrigerator. Get some glasses and plenty of ice. We need something to cope with the heat. Compared to the city, it's cool.

How's Gwen?

Fantastic! She sends her love and thanks for making the wedding so special. We both felt your spirit throughout.

I would not have missed it for the world.

You know how much it meant to us for you just to be there. Even more, Gwen loved the poem you read.

"In the sea of love I melt like salt." I'm glad she liked it.

The other thing that's amazing is that the high I've been on since the wedding is carrying over into work.

Spirit doesn't compartmentalize.

You remember hearing me talk about Jill Stockton?

Maria frowned momentarily. She's your financial VP, right?

That's her. A couple of months ago, she came in with an idea for our next management retreat. Said we should tell stories.

Maria smiled. You were surprised?

Floored. She's good. Brilliant, really. Mostly a number cruncher, though. Funny to hear her suggest we swap stories about the year's highs and lows.

You were pleased?

Beaming! The best thing is, it's not just her. Things like this are popping up all over the place. Team spirit like I'd always hoped for.

What happened with Jill's idea?

A bunch of people got behind it. They made it the centerpiece for our management retreat. We went to this lakeside resort. Beautiful spot. Friday night was the big climax. They'd printed up a fancy program. Billed it as the First Annual Lakeside Lore Hour. All the rules were spelled out in the program.

Rules for what?

For the tournament of tales. Everyone had to share a story at the dinner table. About a peak or a valley from the past year. Then each table chose its best for the finals.

Nominees to compete for the big prize?

Right. In front of the whole group. Even had an applause meter to pick the winner.

Who won?

Would you believe the plant manager in Topeka?

With a story about you?

You remember my side of the story. I thought I'd pulled off a great triumph in modern corporate leadership. His version was different. He billed it as the real story behind the story.

You were embarrassed?

Totally. As he tells it, I wasn't leading them. They were leading me. They had the whole thing scripted beforehand. They felt sorry for me after I got so beat up. They figured I'd blow it unless I got a lot of help. After I left, they had a party. A big celebration of their victory over the boss. Even gave me an award, except I wasn't there to accept it.

What was the award?

How to Lead Without Really Trying.

They were both laughing. It felt good.

A great story, she said.

Everyone thought so. People were falling out of their chairs. The applause pushed the meter off the scale.

How were you feeling?

Stomach in knots. Jaw clamped so tight it was hard to smile convincingly.

Did you get to respond?

Required by the rules. I was tempted to set the record straight. But I exhaled, took a deep breath, and tried to go with the flow. I kept it short. Roasting the boss is probably good for the soul anyway.

True, and a great way to relieve tension between the leader and everyone else.

I said that the stories we shared, even one as outlandish as the winner, were the best gift we could give each other. Each story contained a pearl; a shared ideal, a memory, an insight, a critique, a lesson, a point of pride, a slice of humor. Together our stories summoned and reinforced a common spirit.

How'd they react?

Standing ovation. Not just for me. For everyone there. For our community.

I'm proud of you.

I hoped you would be. You made it possible.

I'm only the midwife. You did the work. And felt most of the pain along the way.

The sun had begun its descent toward a gap in the mountains. A faint breeze began to stir. They looked at each other. He felt a deep connection, a warm tenderness, but mixed with foreboding.

He broke the silence. His mouth felt dry. A feeling of anguish was growing in his heart. The words were hard to say. What I'm feeling now is fear.

So am I.

Their eyes met, bridging the silence. He knew what they needed to talk about. Would she volunteer? Should he ask? He didn't have to wait long for her response.

You know I haven't been well.

For a long time, he replied. Did he mean it as a rebuke? He wasn't sure. He'd felt she was avoiding the subject. It bothered him.

Do you wonder why I didn't tell you before?

Friends talk to friends. If you really believe in giving, why withhold? He sounded harsher than he intended. He saw the flicker of pain in her face and reined himself in.

Her eyes, as bright and intense as ever, never left his. I haven't talked about my health because I hate being a burden on someone I care about. It's easier for me to offer help than take it from others. One of my cardinal imperfections. Anyway, I'm running out of time. You're very important to me. I think of you as a very special legacy.

His anger and guilt had both evaporated. Pushed aside by an overwhelming sense of gratitude and love. That's a big responsibility, he said.

If it's a burden, don't take it.

Not a burden. A gift.

Then enjoy giving it away.

CHAPTER 14

Lifting Our Voices in Song

January. Snow flurries outside his office window. A tough day ahead. Lots of balls in the air. The phone rang. He picked it up.

Is this a good time to talk? she asked.

Perfect, he lied. Thanks for returning my call.

I got your message on the voicemail. You sounded troubled. What's up? she asked.

A classic blooper. It's not easy to screw up the annual holiday party, he said. But somehow we managed.

Easier than you'd think. It's certainly not the first time something that was supposed to be special blew up in someone's face. What happened?

You remember the Lakeside Lore tournament?

How could I forget?

Everyone said it was our best meeting ever. Wonderful feeling of community. But it was only senior management. We all felt that we wanted a wider audience so we could share the spirit with the rest of the staff.

It's a good idea. The problem is pulling it off with the same spirit. Execution is tricky.

We found that out. A group started meeting after the retreat. Called themselves the Lakesiders. They got excited about doing a music video.

Why a music video?

Something to show at our annual holiday fest. You've talked about music as a way to express spirit.

Music is the soul of feelings.

The group pooled their technical skills to produce a musical—*The Holiday Spirit: Our Way of Life.* The video had all the latest bells and whistles—a masterpiece of modern technology.

As a special gift for the holidays?

Seemed like a great idea at the time. Everyone at headquarters came to the party. All the staff. Friends and relatives. You can't believe how much work people put into the production. Making

costumes. Rehearsing nights and
weekends. Renting musicians
from the local symphony.

But something didn't
work?

Artistically, the video
was fantastic. I thought
everyone would love it. Not
true. It flopped.

Do you know why?

Good question. I was stunned.
I introduced the tape myself.
Gave it a big buildup. After that it was
downhill. No enthusiasm. Embarrassing silence. No laughs
at the gag lines. Polite applause at the end. My heart was in
my throat.

It sounds painful.

Excruciating. As the video was winding down I said a quick
prayer for guidance.

Was your prayer answered?

Got help from somewhere. I was at the podium. Panicked.
Trying to figure out what I was going to say to Kurt.

Who's Kurt?

The chief bean counter at corporate. He'd got wind of the musical. He called to tell me it was a dumb way to spend the company's money. I said, "Don't worry, we'll get a big return." He wasn't sold. It's hard to talk spirit to Kurt. He's the kind of guy who'd ask for numbers on the salvation rate before he'd join a church.

I once felt the same about you. Don't write Kurt off too quickly.

Even at my worst I wasn't a penny-pinching control freak like Kurt.

She said nothing. He couldn't actually see her raise her eyebrows and roll her eyes over the phone. But he sensed it.

OK. I'll give Kurt the benefit of the doubt.

So, you're at the podium and the audience is dying on you. Then what?

I started off by thanking everyone who'd worked on the production. Then I asked the audience: "Have you ever watched someone open a gift that you gave them? Then seen them try to hide their disappointment?"

That's a nice analogy.

Seemed to work. I told them you always take a risk when you offer a gift. When it's right, it's glorious. But even if it's not, the same spirit is behind it. That spirit is what our organization is about.

You're getting pretty good at thinking on your feet.

Maybe I'm better at being myself. And speaking from my heart.

Do you know why the video was the wrong gift?

I'm still wrestling with that.

Start with the history. How long has this holiday event been going on?

Years. Way before my time. Same format every year. A lot of people thought it needed a little freshening up.

What was the traditional program?

Open bar. Buffet dinner. Talent show. Sopranos. Barbershop quartets. Harmonicas. Magicians. Employee amateur hour. No talent required. Always seemed to go on forever.

What happened to the amateur hour this year?

Replaced by the video.

And you're still wondering why the effort flopped?

He hoped he didn't sound as sheepish as he felt. I guess it's not much of a mystery. We scrapped a time-honored ceremony. Should have seen it coming.

Why didn't you?

Hubris, I guess. Maybe we got caught up in the moment. The Lakesiders thought we needed something new. The old format was getting tired. People complained all the time.

Did everyone complain? Who did you hear from?

He thought for a moment. I think the Lakesiders and new-comers mostly. Maybe I only heard from the folks who'd already signed on for the new order. Not from those who loved the traditional format.

An important lesson.

Expensive, too. Enough of my woes. How are you?

Physically, not so great. Spiritually, excited. Do you know Rumi called death our wedding with eternity?

No, I never heard that. He felt a chill. Maria's death was hard to face.

And I'm making great progress on my book.

What book?

I've given it a tentative title, *Spiritual Leadership*. You'll enjoy it. You're in it.

In the chapter on what not to do?

No. You're featured in the chapter on spiritual development. I just hope I have time to get the book done.

That's a good incentive to hang around. I have plans for you. Big event coming up in April. I really hope you can come.

What's the occasion?

We're celebrating the company's twenty-fifth anniversary.

I'd love to come. It would be a great honor. But I can't promise.

It was not what he wanted to hear. After saying good-bye, he sat in silence for several minutes, watching the snow fall outside his window. He thought back to the time he had driven through a blizzard to get to her house. He'd do it again in a moment. Would she make it to April? He took time for a prayer.

CHAPTER 15

Celebrating Shared Icons

He was midway through his second cup of coffee. Still basking in memories of the night before. The phone rang. It was Maria. She spoke softly. Her voice weak, raspy.

I'm sorry I missed the anniversary celebration. How was it?

Perfect, except for one thing. You weren't there.

I wanted to be. I just couldn't. Fill me in.

Well, the Lakesiders kept meeting. They put the plan together.

They didn't let the holiday party disaster faze them?

Spurred them on. They were determined to get it right this time. Involved everyone they could. Set up task forces. Amazing what they got done in a couple of months.

Faith moves mountains. Her voice wavered but her conviction came through as clearly as ever.

We had some big ones to move. A lot of loose ends. Time crunch. It's tough linking people on four continents. Kurt was on my neck again about wasting money.

Kurt still has faith in the bottom line.

It's his job.

But it all came together?

Barely. The day before launch, it looked pretty dicey.

It always does.

The plan was simple. Honor the past. Celebrate the present. Look toward the future.

Simple but elegant. You covered the bases.

The history group put together an incredible production. With a perfect theme: *From One Seed, Many Plants*. It opened with John doing a rap song.

John? That's hard to imagine. I've known him since he started the company. He's a wonderful man. But he's a little stiff for rapping. My voice is almost gone, but I might still sing better than John.

He could hear her laughing at the other end of the line. He felt better.

John wasn't too crazy about the costume, either. Plaid shirt. Overalls. Pitchfork. Like American Gothic. You should have heard him, though, in his best scratchy, off-tune baritone. He sounded a little like a German Shepherd growling at the audience. But he put his heart into it—"It was back in Cincinnati that we planted the seed. Tried to build a company I'd be proud to lead."

Unbelievable. Totally out of character for John. She was laughing even harder. I have to see the video.

It's on our website. I'll send you the link.

Good. It should be the best therapy I've had in a long time.

John loved doing it. A vintage performance. Rave reviews.

That's wonderful. He rarely gets that kind of recognition since he retired.

I owe a lot to John. Without his prodding I'd never have come to see you.

It's a mutual debt. What came next?

After John's verse, the camera shifts to the chorus behind him. Out steps the original Topeka plant manager to pick up the lyrics. And it went on like that. Our history. Played out right in front of us in real time. Every era and every site. Very moving.

I can't wait to see it.

The audience was mesmerized. They'd all heard of John. A company legend. But a lot of them had never seen him. Old-timers savored the memories. Newcomers devoured the stories. Everyone loved it.

They usually do. At least when you get the themes right.

So then it was on to the present. We did this round-the-world videoconference. People, places, products. All live. The price tag on that one was a tough sell with Kurt. It was worth it. Even he said so later. First time we could all be at the same party. See each other. Talk to each other. Celebrate together. A big family reunion.

John must have been proud.

It's the first time I ever saw him in tears.

Knowing John, that's remarkable.

He wasn't alone. The feelings were so intense. I was just hoping we could make it through the last part.

The future.

Right. We opened with another video. Young people from around the world. Employees and customers. Talking about their dreams—what they hoped we'd become. The pride they feel in what we're doing on poverty and the environment. Powerful, eloquent, inspired stuff. Reminded me how crazy it was when I thought I was supposed to be the sole source of vision.

You've learned a lot since then. You have the courage now to let others lead.

I needed more courage than that. I was supposed to close off the event.

You had tough acts to follow.

I was too choked up to give my prepared speech. It wouldn't have worked anyway. The young people had said it all.

What did you do?

I talked about you.

You talked about me?

You. I was bone honest. I told them the truth. When I first came into this job, I wasn't ready. I didn't know it at the time, but John did. I told them he put me in touch with a wonderful woman. My spiritual guide. She taught me that leading is giving. That spirit is the core of life. Helped me find my soul. Then I said to the audience: "All of you have been my teachers as well. Together, we're finding the company's soul. We're building an uncommon spirit. One seed, many plants, a shared dream."

Silence on the other end of the line. He knew she was crying.

So was he.

Expressing the Spirit

The most beautiful and profound emotion we can experience is the sensation of the mystical. It is the sower of all true science. He to whom this emotion is a stranger, who can no longer wonder and stand rapt in awe, is as good as dead. To know that what is impenetrable to us really exists, manifesting itself as the highest wisdom and the most radiant beauty, which our dull faculties can comprehend only in their primitive forms—this knowledge, this feeling, is at the center of true religion.

—Albert Einstein[1]

We go to services and read prescribed words, not to find God but to find a congregation, to find other people who are in search of the same divine presence as we are. By coming together, singing together, reading the same words together, we overcome the isolation and solitude with which each of us ordinarily lives. We all become one and we create the moment in which God is present.

—Rabbi Harold Kushner[2]

Steve felt firsthand the costs of walling off spirituality and work. They were at the root of his discouragement when he first visited Maria. His life had become dull and devoid of contour. Devoted to the church of hard work and reason, he paid no attention to his own or his organization's spiritual core. To summon spirit, Steve learned to understand its power and embrace its symbolic discourse: art, ritual, stories, music, and icons.

Expressive activity is integral to meaningful human enterprise. Its absence kills faith and hope. People put in time without passion or purpose. Though fictional, the events in the dialogues are based on direct observations in many successful organizations. Viewed from the outside, the pink Cadillacs, diamonds, and other symbols of Mary Kay Cosmetics may appear superficial and hokey. For insiders, symbols and ceremonies help to anchor the organization's soul and release its spirit.

Story as Public Dream

In his first dialogue with Maria, Steve discovered the magic of stories. Throughout history, people have relied on narrative to express spiritual messages hard to communicate any other way. Successful organizations are storied organizations. One does not have to be there long or go very far to learn the lore. Many contemporary organizations regularly convene times for story-telling. Over time, layers of story accumulate to help people touch the dream world of corporate mythology. Without story and myth, there is no public dream. Without shared dreams, organizations falter and perish. "A dream is a personal experience of that deep, dark mystery that is the support of our conscious lives, and a myth is the society's dream. The myth is the public dream and the dream is the private myth."[3]

Individuals, groups, and organizations all need their own stories. As the artist and author Barry Lopez observes: "Remember only this one thing. The stories people tell have a way of taking care of them. If stories come to you, care for them. And learn to give them away when they are needed. Sometimes a person needs a story—more than food—to stay alive. That is why we put these stories in each other's memories. This is how people care for themselves."[4]

Leaders must venture off the known and protected pathway to find their own private storehouse. Stories help them choose a direction and learn from their experiences. "We tell stories to illuminate the paths we travel, and to share humor, courage, and wisdom in this liberation struggle."[5]

Maria's stories provided a temporary beacon on Steve's path to spiritual liberation, drawing him forward until he could spin tales of his own and help his company along its spiritual path. The winning story at the lakeside retreat, with its moral that leaders need followers, enriched an evolving legend and reminded Steve of a vital leadership lesson: The real drive comes from below.

Music as Enhancement

Steve's venture into music as a way to summon spirit provides an important warning. Expressive activity is powerful. When it works, it is majestic. When it goes awry, it can backfire resonantly, leaving in its wake suspicion, feelings of manipulation, and a sense of betrayal. The composers of the ill-fated musical had a good idea. Their effort misfired because they ignored tradition and lost touch with their audience. The resulting performance evoked disappointment and alienation instead of positive spirit.

Suzanne Langer suggested that music is a symbolic form for conveying feelings and emotions.[6] A movie without music is like food without spice or a summer morning without birds singing in the trees. Music is a language of spirit:

> Words tend to destroy the magic, to desecrate the feelings, and to break the most delicate fabrics of the soul

which have taken this form just because they were incapable of formulation in words, images, or ideas.[7]

Music inspired Steve's epiphany in the Notre-Dame cathedral. The a capella singing was as essential as the majesty of the setting in creating his powerful spiritual experience. The same power of music is essential in modern organizations. Thomas Watson Sr., who made International Business Machines one of the world's most successful companies, understood the importance of singing. IBM used to publish a company songbook so that IBMers of old could sing together. Mr. Watson and the songbook have long since disappeared. It's easy to dismiss the idea of a company songfest as a quaint relic. But viewed as a cultural ritual it helps to explain IBM's fall from grace in the 1980s and subsequent revival in the 1990s with Louis Gerstner at the helm. Gerstner "fell in love" with the company's traditional values and ways and understood better than his immediate predecessor that culture is vital to economic performance: "Culture," he said, "is not just one aspect of the game—it is the game."[8]

Walter Durig, former commander of the Swiss Army, summed it up one evening with a Swiss-German phrase, *"singe oder seckle."* Roughly translated, it says, "Either sing or haul ass."

The Role of History and Icons

Jay Featherstone refers to America as the "United States of Amnesia," because we have so little appreciation of the past. Without roots, plants perish. Without history, the present makes no sense. Without a historical base, a vision is rootless and doomed. Winston Churchill once observed, "The farther backward you look, the farther forward you can see." As Steve came to grips with the gift of significance, he realized the vital role of history in the spiritual life of an organization. In the misguided musical interlude, ignoring history undermined the event. For the twenty-fifth-anniversary celebration, the planners learned from that mistake. As employees around the world reviewed the history of their organization, they strengthened their sense of connection and ownership. His-story became our story. It provided an organic foundation for the present and a launching pad for the future.

To summon spirit, and care for the soul, we must relearn ancient lessons. There is truth beyond rationality. There is another dimension beyond the bottom line. Almost every organization touches this realm from time to time—in retirement parties, holiday gatherings, award banquets, or other special occasions. Too often, such events are last-minute afterthoughts, hastily planned and half-heartedly attended. People see them as they are: mechanical and spiritless, pale reflections of what they could and should be. Absence of spirit exacts a high price. A growing body of evidence confirms that one cost is economic failure.[9] A deeper cost is a loss of significance in a world where everything has a function yet nothing has meaning. Our shrunken psyches are "just as much a victim of industrialization as were the bent bodies of those luckless children who were once confined to English factories from dawn to dusk. . . . Man is essentially festive and fanciful. Celebrating and imagining are integral parts of his humanity but industrial man in the past few centuries has begun to lose his capacity for festival and fantasy. . . . [To regain it, he] must once again learn to dance and to dream."[10] Steve learned firsthand the joys of giving people the opportunity to feel significant. Combining significance with the gifts of love, authorship, and power, he and his associates have grown as leaders and built a spirited, flourishing organization.

A New Life

CHAPTER 16

The Twilight of Leadership

Her call was a surprise. She had never called to request a meeting before. At first he didn't recognize her voice. Even more disturbing, he sensed her purpose. She wanted to say good-bye. He tried to lie to himself. Pretend it was something else. Deep down he sensed the truth.

The familiar road to her house brought back memories. How nervous he'd been the first time they met. The time she told him to get lost, and he did. The many times she had turned his questions back to him—keeping his journey alive and on track. He felt nervous again, but for another reason. When they first met, he was desperate about his life. Now he was fearful for hers. As he pulled up the familiar drive, he hoped to see her standing at the doorway. She wasn't there.

He found her sitting in her favorite chair, cloaked in a colorfully embroidered soft-silk caftan. Her brown eyes seemed even more vivid than he remembered them, her smile as warm and enigmatic as ever. Then he looked more closely. Her eyes seemed more vital only because her face was so pale and thin. There was a hint of sadness that he had never seen before.

I'm so glad you could come, she said softly.

He knew she was making a noble effort to look strong. Her voice gave her away.

You know I can't stay away for long. He tried to sound upbeat.

Thanks for the video presentation. What a wonderful event! I talked to John. He called it a spiritual masterpiece, a work of art. He's very proud. So am I.

You made it possible. Without your—

She held up her hand. I didn't ask you here for that. I need to tell you something. I'm running out of time. This is probably our last meeting.

He knew it was coming, but still wasn't prepared.

I don't know how long I have, she continued. It isn't much. I've been trying to convince myself otherwise.

Me too, for as long as I could. Neither of us can deny it anymore. I wanted us to have some time together before I go. You're very important to me. More than you'll ever know. I love gardening because I love growth. There's great joy in nourishing something and helping it along. It's a lot like parenting. Our time together has been a wonderful gift for me.

He made no effort to resist the feelings that surged from deep inside.

You're the parent I never had, he said. Dad died when I was young. I was close to Mother, but before her death she was a conscience more than a coach. You've been my guide. You're who I want to become.

Her eyes deepened. Do you remember our first meeting? she asked.

Every minute. I thought about it on the drive up. How scared I was. Feeling the bottom dropping out of my life. Nothing made any sense. Nothing I did made things any better.

That happened to me once. A long time ago. Before you were born. Remember how your career was the only thing that mattered? I was the same way. Maybe even more single-minded. It was tough back then, really tough, for a woman. Top jobs went to men. I had to be smarter and work harder. It was the only way to get ahead. I made a lot of sacrifices.

That's why I touched a nerve when I asked about pictures?

Not a nerve. My soul. She stopped and closed her eyes. I only fell in love once. Not wisely, but too well. He was married. I got pregnant. I agonized for weeks. My career or my baby?

He had never felt so much empathy for someone else. Nor so much love. His throat tightened. He swallowed hard. He didn't want to cry. He did anyway.

She waited. Then she continued, haltingly. My heart told me to have the baby. My mind said I couldn't keep it. My heart won. He was a boy. Tommy. She stopped and looked down, tears on her cheeks. Tommy was beautiful. The most wonderful gift I ever received. Then he was gone. SIDS, I guess they'd say now. He's still with me. Every day. No picture on the wall? Seeing him every day would be too painful. He'd be about your age.

Why didn't you tell me? He felt her anguish. He wished he hadn't asked.

She looked down. They sat in silence for several minutes.

At first I didn't make the connection between you and Tommy. If I had, I still wouldn't have told you.

Why not?

That wasn't our agreement. You came for spiritual guidance, even if you didn't know it at first. My job was to help on your journey. Now my journey here is almost over. But there's more I want you to know. After Tommy's death, I tried to lose myself in my career. A lot like you. I got a chance to start my own business. I was lucky—in the right place at the right time. The business became my child. I put everything into making it a success. It worked—beyond my wildest dreams.

I've heard the stories.

There are other things you don't know. Almost no one does.

Why did you leave your business? Wasn't that like giving your child away?

I got sick. Real sick. I was in a lot of pain. I didn't want anyone to know. It was crazy—thinking I couldn't show any weakness. I started using painkillers. I got more addicted to the pills than to my work. I took a long holiday in Europe. That was the cover story. The truth was I checked into a clinic near Paris. I was looking for medical help. I found more than that. There was a priest there—a very wise man. I've never met anyone with a more embracing sense of human spirit. At first he made about as much sense to me as I did to you in our early meetings. But he was patient, and very persistent.

A lot like you.

I hope so. He helped me find a different path.

Like you for me.

After Tommy's death, I'd walled off life's deeper questions. The priest showed me that I had to explore them. When I did, I realized they were more real and more important than anything else. I'd already done what I set out to do in business. My company, my second child, was a success. I'd nurtured my successors. I had enough money. I turned over the business to the next generation. I recreated my life around three passions: art, gardening, and bringing spirit to business leaders.

Helping people like me.

That was my new vocation.

You helped me bring spirit to my company. And my life. It's a debt I can never repay.

You've already paid in full—with interest.

They sat face to face for several minutes. They didn't need to speak. The silence spoke eloquently—two souls joined together. Then a sharp pain appeared to travel across her face, breaking the moment.

He knew her store of energy was gone. He wanted to stay. He knew it was time to leave. He walked over and held her hands. He remembered how comforting her touch had once been for him. He hoped his touch felt comforting to her now. She reached over to the small table nearby. She handed him a small envelope. He recognized her stationery. For later, she said.

Your work will go on, he said, surprised that it came out as a whisper.

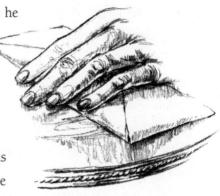

I know. I'll be seeing you.

He barely made it to his car. Biting his lip, he fumbled for his keys. A rush of tears kept him from finding the ignition. He slumped over the steering wheel and cried. *Pull yourself together,* he thought. *What if she's watching?* Then he did the only thing that made any sense. He left the car to walk around the lake.

He came to the stream where he and Maria had once watched a leaf float by. He sat down and opened the envelope. She had handwritten a short note:

Dear Steve,

More than 400 years ago, the great Italian poet Dante gave poetic form to the journey of his own soul. He cast Virgil as his guide through the inferno. At the end of the journey, Virgil takes his leave. Sometimes it's hard

to say what's in our hearts. Virgil's timeless farewell says
what's in mine for you:

You have seen the fires of passion and hell,
My son, and now you arrive
Where I myself can see no further.
I have brought you here by wit and by art.
You take as your guide your heart's true pleasure.
You have passed through the steep and narrow places
And now the sun shines bright
upon your brow.
See around you the flowers and young grasses
which the soil of paradise grows.
Your eyes, whose weeping once
brought me to you,
now shine far and full of bliss.
I can go no further.
Expect from me no further word or sign
Your feel is right, and sound, and free.
To disobey it would be a fault.
Therefore, I give you yourself
crowned and mitered, you are yours.[1]

A flush of love and pride played against his sadness.

CHAPTER 17

Deep Refuge

The funeral was over. He was alone. Still, he felt her presence. He found himself talking to her. Was he crazy? Talking to a ghost? He didn't care.

He remembered the Saturday evening she died. He and Gwen were spending a rare night alone. Sitting, talking, and touching. Jazz in the background. The doorbell was a surprise. Intrusive, unwelcome. It was John. His face said it all. Maria was dead.

Steve remembered putting his arms around John. They'd never hugged before. You'd have been proud, he said.

He remembered the awkwardness. Gwen taking charge. Getting them into the living room. Pouring wine. Asking them to talk about Maria. Stories. Tears. Laughter. Tears again.

He was talking to her now. As if she were there.

At first all I could think about was the void. Who would fill it? How could I go on as a leader without you? Then I realized your spirit is still here, deep in my heart. It always will be, as long as I keep it alive.

I remember going to your house before the memorial service. Everything still there. The garden. The art. On a bedroom table, I found a picture of Tommy. You did keep a photo. Just not on the wall. Maybe it was enough. I wished Tommy could be there. We might have been friends.

He stopped for a while. Sat in silence. It felt strange to be talking with someone who wasn't there. Why? He remembered what he'd learned from her. He talked to her again.

I hope the funeral was what you wanted. Simple. Elegant. From the heart. A reflection of your leadership.

He reviewed in his mind all the stories that her friends had shared. How they came to know her. What she was like. What she had meant to them. Almost everyone had made their own personal offering. He found himself reviewing and savoring John's story more than any other. He tried to see it all in his mind's eye. A hotel ballroom. A big crowd assembled for a testimonial roast in John's honor. A series of roasters, each more irreverent than the last. Then the MC announcing the evening's featured entertainment—direct from Tokyo, Japan's most revered Kabuki player, Marinari Takehashi. An elegant singer in traditional makeup and full kimono padding gently to center stage. A beautiful voice singing Japanese opera. Marinari bowing deeply and walking over to John. Then, to his complete surprise, jumping in his lap and hugging him enthusiastically. John recoiling in shock. Marinari then whispering in his ear, *Hajimemashite.* Gotcha, John-san! John collapsing in laughter when he finally realized that the great Kabuki singer in his arms was none other than Maria.

The entire service had been a beautiful recollection of an extraordinary person. A unique life that enriched so many others.

He spoke to her again.

Maybe you know how much I struggled over what to say. The right words never seemed to come. I'd bought a book of Rumi's poems because you liked them so much. As I reread it, preparing to speak,

the right verse jumped off the page. It said just what I wanted to say.
I hope you heard it.

He recited the poem again, slowly:

> Three companions for you:
> Number one, what you own. He won't even leave
> the house
> for some danger you might be in. He stays inside.
> Number two: your good friend. He at least comes
> to the funeral.
> He stands and talks at the graveside. No further.
> The third companion, what you do, your work,
> goes down into death to be there with you, to
> help.
> Take deep refuge with that companion,
> beforehand.[1]

After I finished, I looked at faces in the audience. I could see their
tears through mine. I knew you were with us.

INTERLUDE 5

The Cycle of the Spirit

Clay lies still, but blood's a rover;
Breath's a ware that will not keep;
Up lad: when the journey's over
There'll be time enough to sleep.

—A. E. Housman[1]

The spiritual cycle has come full circle. In facing Maria's death, Steve begins to anticipate the twilight of his own spiritual journey. Death brings terror. It also brings new life, and renewed appreciation for life's gifts. When we wed, we leave one family to join a new one. When we die, we let go of this world to rejoin eternity.

Embracing Destiny

In *How We Die,* bioethicist Sherwin Nuland reminds us how little we control the timing and the manner of our final exit.[2] When it comes, the end is often messy and painful rather than peaceful and dignified. We know that we will die, but continually seek to push this sobering reality into the shadows of consciousness. The cultural anthropologist Ernest Becker wrote, "Everything man does in his symbolic world is an attempt to deny and overcome his grotesque fate."[3]

The question is whether we must see this fate as grotesque. To deny our destiny is to succumb to fear. To accept it, and to recognize that we contribute through our death as through our life, is liberating. It opens new possibilities for life and leadership.

We usually associate leadership with birth and growth rather than twilight or eclipse. Like all of us, leaders often deny their own mortality, pretending that they or what they have built will last forever.

An old Sufi tale captures this existential burden. It tells of Jesus walking by a flock of sheep and whispering something in the ear of one. Later, that sheep stopped eating and drinking. Several days later, Jesus again passed by the flock and asked the shepherd why the one sheep appeared to be in such poor health. The shepherd, not recognizing Jesus, replied that someone had passed by and whispered something in the sheep's ear. The tale closes with its moral: "If you are curious to know what the venerable Jesus said in the sheep's ear, let me tell you. What the blessed Jesus said was: 'Death exists.' Although it was only an animal, when it heard of death, that sheep stopped eating and went into this state of stupor."[4]

There was a time when Maria's death would have left a gaping wound in Steve's heart and served as a depressing reminder of his own mortality. We have all been stung by the grief and loss following the death of someone we love. Steve's spiritual journey opened a new perspective on death. Finding his own soul opened his heart and enabled him to understand that all of us "are continually dying one another's lives and living one another's deaths."[5] He could now see in death "the poignancy of the transient—that sweet sadness of grasping for something we cannot hold."[6]

Becker finds purpose and even optimism in embracing rather than denying death as the end of life's spiritual journey: "The most that any of us can seem to do is to fashion something—an object or ourselves—and drop it into the confusion, make an offering of it, so to speak, to the life force."[7]

As Steve's personal wounds became the eye to discover his soul, his acceptance of Maria's death opened new possibilities for his leadership. He could now begin each day expecting the unexpected, optimistic that he would find among chaos and confusion opportunities to shape an enduring human institution. He could see more clearly how individual efforts can accumulate into a shared historical legacy. "No matter what he does, every person on earth plays a central role in the history of the world. And normally he doesn't know it."[8]

Choosing Hope

Steve was fortunate to find a guide who challenged and encouraged him to search his heart for leadership possibilities. She helped him move beyond rationality, greed, and the bottom line to discover life's deeper spiritual purpose. The search required him to confront deeply the central questions of meaning and faith: What did he believe? How did he understand the universe and his place in it? He faced the central choice point posited by Andrew Greeley:

> It seems to me that in the last analysis there are only two choices: Macbeth's contention that life is a tale told by an idiot, full of sound and fury and signifying nothing, and Pierre Teilhard's "something is afoot in the universe, something that looks like gestation and birth." Either there is plan and purpose—and that plan and purpose can best be expressed by the words "life" and "love"—or we live in a cruel, arbitrary and deceptive cosmos in which our lives are a brief transition between two oblivions. The data are inconclusive as to these two choices, at least if we look at the data from a rational, scientific standpoint. . . . I opt for hope, not as an irrational choice in the face of the facts, but as a leap of faith in the goodness I have experienced in my life."[9]

As he plumbed his soul, Steve opted for hope. He was able to see gifts of leadership as an expression of life and love, and as a way to help his organization discover a new and vibrant faith. He had become, in Kierkegaard's phrase, a "knight of faith":

> This figure is the man who lives in faith, who has given over the meaning of his life to his creator, and who lives centered on the energies of his maker. He accepts whatever happens in this visible dimension without complaint, lives his life as a duty, faces his death without qualms. No pettiness is so petty that it threatens his meaning; no task is too frightening to be beyond his courage. He is fully in the world on its terms and wholly beyond the world in his trust of the invisible dimension. The knight of faith then represents what we call an ordeal of mental health, the continued openness of life out of the death throes of dread.[10]

Seeking Wisdom

America's nineteenth-century captains of industry led their organizations to international preeminence. Captains of industry were gradually replaced by modern managers who have helped us see the virtues of clear goals, measurable objectives, specialization, standards, and accountability. We have come a long way from our ancestors who worked intimately with nature in families and small communities. We face challenges today that fall beyond the reach of the captains of industry and modern management. Technological advances have created previously unknown conveniences and efficiencies. Yet we still face an onslaught of problems—such as alienation, malaise, violence, and poverty—that are frustratingly recalcitrant in the face of rational and technical solutions.

More and more of us see that many of those problems are rooted in a disease of the human spirit. One American president after another has echoed this concern. Jimmy Carter may have been ahead of his time when he suggested that America was suffering from a spiritual malaise. Few of his countrymen thanked him at the time, but Bill Clinton returned to the same theme fifteen years later. Nor is this a message restricted to Baptists, southerners, or Democrats. Lee Atwater, one of the architects of Ronald Reagan's political success, talked about the "spiritual vacuum in the heart of the American society, this tumor of the soul." In another niche of American society, the same message was echoed by a self-described "unemployed, impoverished, chronically-ill, disabled and usually homeless" man in Nashville. He wrote in the editorial page of the local newspaper, "Our nation is having a severe and major spiritual crisis in which the future of the country is in great danger."

To prevail in the face of our spiritual challenges, we need a vision of leadership rooted in an enduring sense of human wisdom. We need a new generation of seekers—the Marias and Steves who have the courage to confront their own demons, to embark upon a personal quest for spirit and heart, and the commitment to share their learning and gifts with others.

How will we develop the seekers that we need? To begin with, we need a revolution in how we think about leadership and how we develop leaders. Management and leadership development programs often ignore or demean spirit. They need an infusion of soulful forms like poetry, literature, music, art, theater, history, philosophy, and dance. We also need more Marias—guides who can encourage us on our journey and help us to learn from our experience—including our failures. In recent decades, we have evolved a kind of implicit compact with the most senior members of our community. In return for better medical care and more financial independence, they are expected to go off to play bridge or golf, leaving the rest of us to get on with our own pursuits. The implicit message is that we want them to be comfortable, even though they are largely useless. We have thus cordoned off potential sources of spiritual insight in retirement homes and communities where their wisdom and experience are rarely available to the rest of us.

Leaders like Steve often find themselves confronting awesome challenges with inadequate reservoirs of experience or seasoning. They look to books, articles, consultants, and workshops to find the latest solution-in-good-standing. When those fail, they turn to the next fad. Yet there are countless potential Marias in the world—sources of guidance who are untapped or underused. A return to spirituality will lead us to seek their wisdom. In matters of spirit, wisdom and experience count far more than technique or strategy.

Like Maria, great spiritual teachers from many cultures and traditions have believed that their task is to help seekers find wisdom from within rather than without. This message is the central point of a story told repeatedly in many different spiritual traditions. The poet and mystic Andrew Harvey offers a Sufi rendition of the tale:

> There was a man who lived in Istanbul, a poor man. One night he dreamed vividly of a very great treasure. In a courtyard, through a door, he saw a pile of blazing jewels heaped by the side of an old man with a beard. In the dream, a voice told him an address, 3 Stassanopoulis Street, Cairo. Because he had learned enough to trust his dream visions, he went on a long

arduous journey to 3 Stassanopoulis Street in Cairo. One day, many years later, he came to that doorway, entered through it into a courtyard full of light, saw the old man from his dream sitting on the bench, went up to him, and said, "I had a dream many years ago, and in the dream I saw you sitting exactly where you are sitting now, and I saw this great heap of treasure by you. I have come to tell you my dream and to claim my treasure." The old man smiled, embraced him, and said, "How strange, I had a dream last night that under a bed in a poor house in Istanbul there was the greatest treasure I have ever seen." At that moment, the poor man saw that what he had been looking for all those years was really under his own bed, in his own heart, at the core of his own life.[11]

The responsibility of the guide is not to give answers, but to raise questions, suggest directions to explore, and to offer support. "Man is reborn, no longer born of the flesh, but reborn of the spirit, of the inspiration from within and the teacher without."[12]

If we look for guidance, no doubt we can find it, but we need to choose wisely. There is always the risk of false prophets—

charismatic figures like Marshall Applewhite, Jim Jones, David Koresh, and all the other abusive priests and political or spiritual leaders who have exploited followers and perverted faith. We should be profoundly skeptical of anyone who offers a faith built on exclusivity, isolation, and intolerance. But there are many teachers whose spirituality is solidly rooted in love and wisdom. Their faith may help us reclaim and regain our souls. Once we find our own light within, we can share it with others, offering gifts from our heart. Gifts of love, authorship, power, and significance can create the robust, spirited organizations we need.

CHAPTER 18

The Legacy

A month later, Steve was at his desk, wondering what was on Jill Stockton's mind. It's personal, she'd said, when she asked to meet. His reverie was soon interrupted. Jill was there. No trace of her usual cheerful smile.

She took a seat. He waited for her to take the lead.

It's your fault, she said. I was fine until you started all this talk about spirit.

And now?

It always seemed pretty straightforward. I worked hard in college. Did well in business school. My career is going well. I'm a really good finance officer.

One of the best, he said.

My marriage is great. The kids are thriving. So why am I starting to ask what's life all about?

A wake-up call. From your soul.

Soul? I don't even know what the word means.

That explains the call.

So do I pick up the phone and say, "Is that you, soul?"

Might work. But you don't really need a phone. You need to look inside yourself.

Meaning what?

Listen to your heart.

She glanced briefly toward the door.

Are you thinking you should break for the exit before I say something even crazier?

She laughed and relaxed a little. How'd you know?

I've been there.

I'm good with numbers. When you tell me to look inside, listen to my heart, I don't even know where to begin.

How often do you pray?

She stared at him, a look of surprise spreading across her face. He could see she didn't expect the question.

When she spoke, the words came slowly. I don't. Who would I pray to?

Maria taught me that prayer is a heartsong. It's one way to talk to your soul.

And what is my soul supposed to tell me?

Maybe that the only place you can find what you're looking for is in the cave you're afraid to enter.

Jill fell into startled, uncharacteristic silence. Then, as she stared at Steve, her mouth slowly relaxed into a smile. In my dreams it's not a cave. It's a dark room. Someone's after me, and that dark room is the only way to escape. But I'm too scared to go in. So I'm trapped.

I used to feel the same way. That's what took me to Maria.

You found what you were looking for?

And much more.

So can you give me a preview of what's ahead?

I can't tell you what's in your heart. Only you can do that.

He smiled as he remembered his first meeting with Maria. She'd told him the same thing. *To everything a season*, he thought, *and a time to every purpose*. Time now to help someone else on her journey.

Postlude

Soul at Work

In the real world, are there leaders like Maria and Steve? Are there workplaces that take soul and spirit seriously? Absolutely, but some have doubts. "I love the idea of more soulful and spirited workplaces," one Dutch reader told us, "but this vision might be too beautiful for this hard world." A reader in California commented, "The book describes a leader with strong spiritual convictions, giving and loving. But, how such a leader can survive the harsh business reality is not clear to me." Skepticism comes as no surprise. Business realities are often harsh and many executives still don't see beyond the bottom line. Yet a growing list of examples shows that a spiritual renaissance in the workplace is not only possible, it's already happening.

Take Ari Weinzweig and Paul Saginaw, who founded
Zingerman's Deli in Ann Arbor, Michigan, with a simple goal of
serving the world's best sandwiches. They did that and more,
but not without struggle. As Bo Burlingham tells the story, the
runaway success of their deli led to a major debate between
the founders.[1] Saginaw wanted to expand to new locations.
Weinzweig said flatly that he didn't "want to spend time flying
to Kansas City to see some mediocre Zingerman's."[2] They eventually found a path they could both agree on: create a series of
hometown businesses, each with its own distinctive identity.
They developed more than ten members of the "Zingerman's
Community of Businesses," all based in Ann Arbor. Among them
were a bakery, candy shop, coffee house, creamery, book publisher, retail website, and consulting firm. Meanwhile, they also
expanded into the nonprofit world, beginning with Food
Gatherers, a local organization founded by Paul Saginaw to
locate food that would otherwise be thrown away and distribute
it to people who needed it. That led to a number of other nonprofits, and Saginaw eventually took on the title of chief spiritual
officer, devoting as much as twenty-five hours a week to
nonprofits and community activities. Why? In Saginaw's eyes,
contributing to the community isn't an extracurricular activity,
it's one of the main reasons they're in business. "It's a joy," he

says. "Being in the community like that is a joy. You can't buy joy."[3]

Can spiritual leadership also work in businesses that don't cater to upscale consumers in an affluent college town? Here's another example, from the Kansas City *Star* a few years back:

A couple of years ago, Ford plant manager Gerry Minor began holding Friday afternoon leadership meetings to share information and management training. Anyone in the plant is welcome to attend. Regular features include a "business acumen" presentation that shares financial or business information. Last week's session, for example, emphasized the financial imprint of the plant, which employs 4,880 hourly and 342 salaried workers.

Also on the agenda are discussions of reading material Minor assigns. Last week the focus was on *Leading with Soul,* an allegory about a search for meaning in life and work, written by Lee Bolman and Terry Deal.

Joe Williams, a financial analyst who spent 11 years on the assembly line before getting a college degree and moving into the plant's finance office, wore a tux as the book report's master of ceremonies.

"We wanted to have fun," Williams said of the reviewers, who were first-line supervisors and midlevel plant managers. They read the book and shared their reactions, interspersed with "Sister Act" clips showing the step-by-step transformation of a dismal choir into crowd-pleasing performers.

When Minor first convened the Friday afternoon meetings, those who attended were quiet and came mostly to observe. Over the months, staff involvement has grown. Inhibitions have waned.

"We have seen the power of shared emotion, of creating a common spirit," Minor said after the review group's presentation. Minor wouldn't mind if shared spirit is his legacy at the plant, which became Ford's largest-volume manufacturing site under his tenure.[4]

You might have thought that an old Ford plant in Claycomo, Missouri, would be one of the last places in the world to put *Leading with Soul* on its reading list. Yet that kind of unorthodox approach helped Claycomo become one of the largest and most successful auto plants in the world. It's not an isolated example. Since *Leading with Soul* was first published, we've received calls and letters from people all over the world who were getting together with coworkers to explore the implications of the book for their own organization. Among them were a hotel in Jakarta, an oil company in Texas, a nonprofit in Michigan, and a consumer products company in Japan.

We have also been gratified by enormous interest in spiritual issues that we have found in school districts across America. One fascinating example is in Lawndale, California. The Lawndale Elementary District might seem an unlikely candidate for a spiritual renaissance. It is in a poor town just south of the Los Angeles airport, and 91 percent of its students are minorities, 84 percent receive free or reduced lunches, and 20 percent are transitory. To make things even more difficult, the district's staff is mostly white.

Several years ago, the superintendent, Dr. Joe Condon, and one of the district's principals, Dorinda Dee, got together after the summer recess. Each had a book to recommend to the other. They were surprised to learn that their recommendations were identical—*Leading with Soul.* The superintendent soon bought the book for each of the system's principals. The leadership team used it as a basis for a series of discussions.

The first part of the group's discussion centered on personal journeys. "The book became a tool to look at ourselves and then at how we could connect more closely to our lives at work. We realized that when you tap into your soul you realize that you have personal gifts to share and then can offer them to the wider community." From the leadership team, the ideas began to migrate into the Lawndale culture. Some of the discussions were one-on-one, others were in small groups. Teachers especially were drawn into the discussions. "Teachers have life issues going on when teaching. If a teacher dries up, he or she can't help others. People learned they have to take care of themselves to do a good job. The real meaning of leading with soul is what teaching is all about. Maria was Steve's teacher." Just before his retirement, the superintendent summed up the emerging spirit of Lawndale: "In my annual report to the school board, not one word was spent on goals or test scores. We focused on what people are bringing to the party. This goes much deeper than work. It gets at the essence of who we are. We have to deal with that before we start to work."[5]

Condon was succeeded in 2009 by Dr. Ellen Dougherty, but an emphasis on caring and soul persists. She says, "This is our way of bringing the whole side of life into balance—caring, authorship, and power give significance to what we do. To work is to live; to live is to work."

Bringing soul to work is not just an American phenomenon. Examples are proliferating around the world. Our colleague Philip Mirvis was kind enough to share his experiences in working with a fascinating company in the Netherlands:

> When Tex Gunning took charge in late 1995 of Van den Bergh Foods, a Dutch subsidiary of Unilever, he made all the right moves: an analysis of current problems and opportunities, the start of a bold change program to turn around lackluster performance, and the launch of successful new products. But something was missing. At a management meeting in late 1997 participants agreed that business was good, but the company lacked "heart." Their aspiration was to reconnect deeply—intellectually and emotionally—to each other and to customers.
>
> Working with me and a team of group facilitators from the Foundation for Community Encouragement, Tex led a series of retreats with roughly 200 leaders at all levels in the company. In 1998, all 200 bicycled and camped together in the Ardennes Forest in Belgium. In an ancient

monastery, Tex shared his emotional lifeline—a story of experiences, both highs and lows—from childhood to the present. Leaders then shared their own stories with two or three peers. In the next two days, they met in moments of silent reflection and in open dialogues about their work and the business. A collective commitment was made to "be authentic" with one other, to listen deeply, and to "deal with difficult issues."

As a follow-up, the 200 participated in a company-wide learning conference with all 2400 of their employees, who also shared life histories and talked about themselves and their work. One manager summed up the impact: "For me it represented a major turnaround . . . the way leaders and then all the people of Van den Bergh showed something personal about themselves. The example showed that I am more than just a 'working' person in the company. The 'whole' person is welcomed."

Gunning's next stop was as president of Unilever's food group in Asia. He was confident that he could fulfill his charge of building the business, but he saw something even more difficult and important to do: save the lives of children all over Asia who were dying from health and nutrition deficiencies. As Gunning put it:

Good leaders take care of themselves, their families, and some of the community. Great leaders—and great companies—not only take care of these stakeholders but also want to change the world. They want to leave the world better than they found it. We have made the choice to have our business intent become a missionary intent that will make a difference in the lives of Asians who have either health problems, nutritional problems, or well-being problems.[6]

In 2004 Unilever CEO Patrick Cescau appointed Gunning to head a task force to examine the company's global approach to corporate citizenship. Unilever's corporate mission called for adding "vitality to life by meeting everyday needs for nutrition, hygiene and personal care brands that help people feel good, look good, and get more out of life."[7] Gunning's task force proposed integrating citizenship into the vitality mission, and aligning all of Unilever's brands with an expanded commitment to adding vitality to society. With more than 400 brands, 160,000 employees, and revenues above $50 billion in 2009, Unilever had become one of the largest consumer products companies in the world. Its social footprint and potential leverage, for good or ill, were enormous. The company concluded that, in the long run, business success and social impact had to go hand in hand. With strong CEO backing, Unilever created a unified Corporate Social Responsibility reporting structure, and introduced social and environmental criteria into the brand development process, creating "a value proposition for bringing Unilever's new generation model of citizenship to the marketplace."[8]

These are only a few examples of individuals and organizations evolving their own distinctive approaches to leading with soul. In many of those efforts we see leaders offering their unique versions of the four gifts discussed in the book—authorship, love, power, and significance.

The Gift of Authorship

For Ray Anderson, the founding CEO of Interface Carpet, the epiphany came in the mid-1990s after he read Paul Hawken's influential *Ecology of Commerce*.[9] By the time he put down the book, Anderson could not escape the uncomfortable conclusion that he and his firm were environmental criminals, participants in an unsustainable cycle of extraction, manufacture, and waste. He took a dramatic leap of faith, convening a task force and charging the group to find ways to reinvent the business to make it environmentally sustainable. Many people both inside and outside of his business thought Anderson was naive or crazy, but he was convinced that the company's business model was flawed—"turning petrochemicals into carpets that last ten years and then spend up to twenty thousand years in landfills." The initiative evolved into "Mission Zero": the goal of eliminating any negative impact on the environment by 2020. Doubters wondered if Interface was off on a romantic detour to financial ruin, but Anderson's confidence paid off:

> For the shareholders, costs are down, not up, dispelling a myth and exposing the false choice between environment and economy. Products are the best ever, as design for sustainability has proven to be a wellspring of innovation. People are galvanized around a shared higher purpose. And the goodwill of the marketplace is amazing. No amount of clever marketing at any cost could have created as much.[10]

A key to the success of the Interface sustainability initiative was widely shared authorship. In his initial charge to the sustainability task force, Anderson provided a broad goal of achieving sustainability, but left it to the group to figure out when and how. He chose to "pass ownership of the sustainability strategy from himself, as the visionary, to his audience, the implementers. He looked to employees, suppliers, shareholders, and even customers for necessary ideas, solutions, and support rather than choosing a course of action by himself and directing others to follow."[11] The results were dramatic; change began to bubble up everywhere. Plant managers found ways to re-use scrap material previously tossed. The sales team came up with a powerful and novel idea: instead of selling carpet, Interface could lease it and take it back at the end of its cycle so that the materials could be reused. It turned out that Interface found better ways to reduce expenses as people throughout the organization focused on saving the planet instead of cutting costs.

University classrooms are often places where the teacher issues commands students dutifully follow. "Do what you are told, work hard, and a good grade will be your reward." Too often, this results in assignments students hate doing and their instructors hate grading. But one professor found that surprising things happened when he tried to offer authorship to a group of students enrolled in a senior seminar:

> Year after year, I've given students specific instructions
> for the assignments I'd ask them to do. They would
> comply, and I would feel in complete control. But they

never seemed really excited about what they were doing. And I was rarely very impressed with what they had done. *Leading with Soul* offered a new possibility: why not give them a chance to create something on their own. So rather than a specific assignment, I gave them a rather amorphous task—a reflective essay. But as time went on, I was disappointed in the results. No one seemed to be doing anything. As the semester drew to a close, I grew more and more angry. At the last class, I decided to vent my frustration. The students had taken advantage of my gift and I wanted them to know how it felt to be ripped off.

As I was preparing to launch my diatribe, one of the students raised her hand and asked when they could share their personal growth projects. I told her I did not assign a personal growth project. She told me the class had gotten together and figured out what I really meant by reflective essay. They then shared what they had done.

I was completely blown away by their accomplishments: art, poetry, and other attempts to capture the essence of leadership. One student remarked that he learned that leadership was as much about reflection as about action. His personal growth project was to design and build a bench where students could sit and reflect because he had observed that there was no place like that on campus. That bench is now a popular spot where students can sit and ponder the meaning of life. Another student was disturbed about a University tradition that had been discarded. When her mother graduated, students received an Iris bulb as a symbol that their knowledge would continue to grow. Her mother's bulb eventually become a large Iris bed that was a source of family pride. As her personal growth project, the student asked some wealthy graduates of the University for donations to make it possible for each of the graduating seniors to receive an iris during commencement. Her efforts became part of a front page article in the University newspaper. When that news came to the attention of the faculty commencement committee she was summoned to appear. Her plan flew in the face of a University rule that prohibited any kind of adornment at graduation. But she was determined and willing to risk whatever punishment would befall her if she carried out her plan.

The day of graduation the seniors marched in carrying their beautiful blue irises. During his speech, the University chancellor commented on what the student had done and read a letter from an alumnus whose heart had been deeply moved by the renewal of an old tradition. As he spoke, all the seniors raised their irises high. The student's personal growth project had made a real difference. Later on, the student called me and asked if she had learned the right lesson from her experience: "As a leader you do what you think is right and stand prepared to take the heat so that good things can happen." Those are only two examples of what the gift of authorship yielded. Even in my wildest dreams I would never have imagined what students could do if given the chance.

The same lesson applies to employees, wherever they work. Following the rules and doing what you're told pales in significance to what people can do when given the opportunity to put their signature on their work. More and more companies are now taking notice: cut employees some slack, encourage them to think, and watch what they can do on their own without direction from the top.

The Gift of Love

If you doubt that love can have a place in a modern corporation, try telling it to Herb Kelleher, the one-of-a-kind founder and CEO-emeritus of Southwest Airlines. When asked what made Southwest so successful, Kelleher always talked about people, humor, love, and soul. Even after he retired, they continued to talk openly about love at Southwest Airlines. They fly out of Love Field in Dallas; their symbol on the New York Stock Exchange is LUV; the employee newsletter is called *Luv Lines;* and their twentieth anniversary slogan was "20 Years of Loving You."[12] Like everyone in the industry, Southwest experienced a steep downturn after 9/11, but it was the only U.S. airline that laid no one off. Every airline would love to match Southwest's success, but most don't understand how it was achieved nor how to match a culture that produces the lowest employee turnover and highest customer satisfaction in the industry.

Many other successful leaders and organizations embrace a philosophy much like Kelleher's. Etta Erickson, a manager at Healtheast, a hospital group in Minnesota, saw love as a central feature in her organization: "There's real compassion and love and relationship in this organization; there's friendship, there's support, there's trust."[13] In Healtheast's culture, the phrase "moments of truth" is used to describe encounters that let patients and their families form impressions of the quality of the organization's service. Employees remind each other that every moment of truth has the potential to become a "moment of compassion."[14]

In 1980, Doris Christopher borrowed $3,000 to start a home-based business selling cooking utensils. More than two decades later, she sold her wildly successful Pampered Chef to Warren Buffett. Buffett described it as the kind of business he loved to buy because Christopher and her management team "clearly love the business and the people they work with."[15] From the beginning, Christopher emphasized taking care of her sales representatives, the "kitchen consultants" who went into people's homes to demonstrate the products. But she went further by expanding the concept of love beyond her business. Deeply troubled that millions of Americans didn't have enough to eat, Christopher and Pampered Chef began in the 1990s to partner with Second Harvest, the largest network of food banks in the United States. Pampered Chef's "Round-up from the Heart" initiative began as a holiday program, but eventually expanded to year-round. By encouraging customers to round up their purchases to the nearest dollar, the company was able to parlay thousands of tiny donations into a single donation of more than a $1 million a year to Second Harvest.[16]

Gift of Power

It takes faith in your people to see empowerment as a formula for success, but examples of organizations that have made the leap are multiplying. You can see it in many of the companies that make *Fortune*'s annual list of the "100 Best Places to Work in America." The gift of power is central to the "open book management" movement, inspired particularly by Jack Stack of Springfield Remanufacturing. Stack tells a persuasive story of turning around a moribund manufacturing company in Missouri by giving employees as much financial information as possible so that they began to think and act like owners. Stack's "ultimate higher law" is that you get the highest performance when you appeal to the highest level of thinking. The success of that philosophy has since been replicated in many other organizations.[17]

Recreational Equipment Inc. (REI), a customer-owned co-op, has grown from a single store in Seattle in 1938 to a retail powerhouse with more than a hundred outlets. The success formula puts strong emphasis on empowering employees to take care of customers. Flexible hours, telecommuting, bringing your dog to work, and wearing whatever you want are all part of the culture. After fifteen years you get a sabbatical, and another one every five years thereafter. One REI sales specialist commented that the thing that most distinguished the company from anyplace else he'd worked was that he was "empowered to be honest with the people I help."

An even more dramatic example of giving power to employees can be found in Brazilian manufacturer Semco.[18] Ricardo Semler took over the company from his father in the 1980s and set about transforming its autocratic culture into an unorthodox philosophy of management:

- The key to management is to get rid of all the managers.
- The key to getting work done on time is to stop wearing a watch.
- The best way to invest corporate profits is to give them to the employees.
- The purpose of work is not to make money. The purpose of work is to make the employees, whether working stiffs or top executives, feel good about life.[19]

At Semco, workers hire new employees, evaluate bosses, and vote on major decisions. In one instance, employees voted to purchase an abandoned factory that Semler didn't want and then proceeded to turn it into a remarkable success. Semco's experiments produced dramatic gains in productivity, and the company was repeatedly rated the best place to work in Brazil. Even after Semler no longer saw a need for his company to grow, it grew anyway because innovative employee groups kept inventing new businesses.

One of the most subtle but profound examples of an organization that has discovered how to use the gift of power is Alcoholics Anonymous. AA's twelve-step program has achieved extraordinary success in helping addicts escape alcohol dependence. Its emphasis on spirituality has worked where professionalism and expertise have repeatedly failed. AA gives power paradoxically. The first of its twelve steps asks addicts to acknowledge, "We are powerless over alcohol, and our lives have become unmanageable." The second step is to accept that there is a "Power greater than ourselves" that could "restore us to sanity." The third is to turn "our wills and our lives over to the care of God as we understand him." The eleventh step asks the addict to pray "only for knowledge of His will for us and the power to carry that out." The path to power, in AA's view the *only* path, begins with admitting powerlessness and putting oneself in the hands of a higher power. But AA does not expect individuals to find and follow this path on their own. They learn from other recovering addicts. In AA, everyone teaches and everyone learns. Each individual must rely on a higher power, but each is a medium for empowering others.

Modern organizations are increasingly recognizing the power of AA's basic message. The more individuals try to go it alone and rely solely on themselves, the more powerless they will be. The path to power and empowerment requires deep understanding that each of us is finite and needs help from those around us.

The Gift of Significance

Many business executives still cling to a simpler world in which the bottom line is the only thing that really matters. But smart leaders and progressive companies understand that long-term success requires a larger view of what's important, including a broader sweep of stakeholders. Nike and its enigmatic CEO Phil Knight faced this challenge in the late 1990s amid a flood of bad publicity about the "Sneaker Gulag." The dreadful pay and working conditions of the mostly Asian workers who produced most of Nike's shoes damaged the brand and the business. After denial and defense failed, Nike realized it needed to bring its creative talent to bear on its supply chain. It worked on promoting responsible practices end to end—from factories in Asia to retailers in the United States. It worked to improve conditions both in its plants and the surrounding communities. It supported a global alliance that worked to improve education and health for workers in Asia, and it launched its own education programs in China.[20] It developed metrics for the environmental impact of all its products. Mark Parker, CEO since 2006, has become one of the most visible business champions of sustainability.

In reflecting on a history that included both ups and downs, IBM realized that "it had been most successful when its values were strong and its employees were aligned with them."[21] In 2003, IBM CEO Sam Palmisano initiated an online "ValuesJam" that engaged almost the entire company in a debate and redefinition of core values. "This jam lasted for seventy-two hours and has been described variously as 'freewheeling,' 'passionate,' and 'brutally honest.' The contributors debated whether or not company values existed and how they were established. They talked about the values IBM needed to be successful and the unique contribution IBM could make to the world. In a virtual room dedicated to positive thinking, they also talked about what made them proud of IBM when the company was at its best."[22] Three core values emerged from the conversation:

dedication to customers' success, innovation that matters for the company and the world, and trust and personal responsibility in all relationships.

Medtronic, a highly successful multinational health care firm, like many successful organizations, looks beyond the bottom line to focus on its deeper mission. That mission gives significance to everything Medtronics' people do. In his insightful book, *Leading Consciously,* our colleague Debashis Chatterjee quotes Bill George, the chief executive of Medtronic, on the firm's spiritual underpinnings:

> Medtronics was founded by a spiritual leader named Earl Bakken. Earl is still the spiritual leader, or "soul" of Medtronic, despite the fact that he has been retired for four years.
>
> The mission he wrote more than thirty years ago, not one word changed, calls for Medtronic to restore people to the fullness of life and health. Our 9,000 employees are totally dedicated to that mission, regardless of whether they work in the R&D lab, the factory, the accounting department, or in the hospital. What are these values? They are, first of all, restoring people to full health; next, serving our customer with products

and services of unsurpassed quality; recognizing the personal worth of employees; making a fair profit and return for our shareholders; and maintaining good citizenship as a company. . . . And the results of the past thirty years, or the past eight years, seem to validate that approach: $1,000 invested in 1960 in Medtronic stock would be worth $1.65 million today. At Medtronic, we don't mix religion and business, but we certainly do not shy away from the spiritual side of our work and the deeper meaning of our mission to save lives.[23]

Significance may be relatively easy to define in the health care business, but what if your work is less glamorous? We've already described how the sustainability mission gave new meaning and inspiration to everyone at Interface Carpet, and how Tex Gunning and colleagues at Unilever's Asia foods business built significance around a mission of developing better ways to feed poor children. What about a business built around cows? Seven of them for Gary Hirshberg, who started in 1983 with that little herd, a dilapidated Vermont barn, a yogurt recipe, and dreams of saving the earth. In the early going he was on a fast track to burnout and failure, but eventually the business developed into the leading brand of organic yogurt, Stonyfield Farms. The formula for success, as Christine Arena described it in her book *Cause for Success,* was all about a larger purpose:

> Stonyfield isn't just a company that sells yogurt. It also fosters optimism about the way food is used and produced, about the meaning of corporate activism, and about the future. Hope is the core value of the company, and through the bulk of its activities Stonyfield translates this value into winning business approaches that improve public health, increase farmer prosperity, and detract from global warming.[24]

Conclusion

There are a growing number of examples both in business and elsewhere of organizations exploring soul and spirit in ways that create bonds, kindle passion, and give meaning to work. Organizations are finding unique and creative ways to offer gifts like authorship, power, love, and significance.

Sometimes, all it takes is a simple act of caring by one individual. Our friend John Jacobson shared a simple but powerful example:

> When I was a principal, a first-grade child, Cheryl, lost her mother to cancer. As she dealt with this tragic loss,

she turned to writing as a source of comfort and an outlet of her feelings and emotions. Upon completion of her writing, the teacher asked Cheryl if she wanted to share her writing with the class. In this first-grade classroom the sharing of writing was an everyday occurrence at the end of the writing workshop. During this sharing time, children generally sat in an author's chair in the front of the class with children gathered around on the carpet. On this particular day, the teacher, being sensitive to Cheryl's feelings, asked her if she would like to sit on his lap. As Cheryl shared her thoughts with the class, secure in her teacher's lap, hearts were touched and the class bonded in spirit.

All four gifts were exchanged in one simple encounter. What better way to experience authorship than to sit in the author's chair and share one's own writing? The offer of a lap to sit on exemplifies the possibilities for love that we often miss in daily life. Writing about one's feelings and experiences, and sharing them with friends, are a powerful way to find meaning and significance. For this child, they helped her begin to exert some power over the demons that were haunting her.

The possibilities are all around us if we look for them. Sometimes all it takes is a simple gesture. At others, it will require all the passion, courage, and caring we can muster. But the examples discussed in this chapter suggest that the rewards are great.

"I wear the chains I forged in life," says Marley's ghost in Charles Dickens's *A Christmas Carol.* Each of us each day builds our legacy, our contribution to humankind. Though we may not admit it even to ourselves, many of us live as if hoping to be remembered for the size of a house, the nameplate on a car, or a rung attained on a corporate ladder. Small wonder so many successful people, like Steve Camden in our story, hit a wall and wonder what happened to the meaning and zest in their lives. The world will little lament nor long remember those whose primary life achievement is material comfort or self-aggrandizement.

The message of this book is simple. Your life journey is a continuing opportunity to deepen your faith, develop your gifts, and enhance your contribution to what the world becomes. At Maria's funeral (in Chapter Seventeen), Steve Camden read Rumi's poetic description of three companions. The first, your possessions, won't even leave the house when you're in danger or difficulty. The second, your good friend, will come to the funeral, but not further. Only the third, your work—all that you do to offer your unique gifts to others—goes beyond this life "down into the grave, to help." Rumi's advice is sound: take deep refuge with that companion beforehand. David Batstone captures the immediate concern: "At this moment the corporation sorely needs leaders—not people with titles, but true leaders at every level of the corporate ladder—to live with soul. . . . I am inclined to believe, however, that for most people, it is not a new path but the truth about themselves that awaits discovery. Once they start living out of that discovery, they inspire everyone around them."[25]

Continuing a Spirited Dialogue

In the first editions of *Leading with Soul,* we invited readers to share their experiences of integrating soul into their lives at work and at home. We are grateful to the many who responded and shared accounts from their life journeys. Letters came from all over the world and across economic sectors. Responses were rich, moving, and varied. Many readers posed provocative questions that we had not considered as we wrote the book. Here we share some readers' questions and offer responses drawn from our own experience and from the many stories that readers have shared.

We begin with questions about the book itself: Why did we write it, and what were our hopes for it? Then we take on some specific and personal how-to questions. These have often taken the form, "Sure, it sounds good, but how do I actually do it? How can I put any of these ideas into practice?" Finally, we discuss some questions that move beyond personal spirituality to focus on issues of spiritual development in the larger world: What's happening now, and what might happen in the future?

Queries About the Book

Why did you write about spirit and soul?

We wrote the book for our readers and for ourselves. We hoped to buoy readers in their search for meaning and faith. But we also wrote it for ourselves because it was what we needed to do, even if we didn't know it when we started. The process embarked us on individual journeys that have intertwined and diverged at various times over the last several decades. We have learned much from one another and from the personal search and reflection that were integral to our writing process.

Did you consciously choose Maria at the outset as the spiritual guide?

Maria evolved as we wrote. She began as a nameless, white-bearded, hermitlike *he*. But our hermit didn't seem to be up to the job—he lacked warmth and heart. Maria gradually took shape, evolving into a fuller person as the story developed. Adam and Eve, Mars and Venus exist in all of us. That helps explain why we needed our spiritual guide to be a woman, whereas Susan Trott, in her wise and delightful book *The Holy Man*, chooses a male as her title character.[1] Maria made our story work and helped us explore the feminine and the masculine in ourselves.

What makes leading with soul and spirit different from other leadership perspectives that emphasize compassion, collaboration, and ethics?

It comes down to the difference between asking "What works?" and "What matters?" The tension between the two is illustrated in Bowen McCoy's "Parable of the Sadhu," in which he relates an experience during a high-altitude hike in the Himalayas.[2] As he neared the highest point of a multiday trek, he and his hiking partner encountered a pilgrim, a Sadhu, who was lightly dressed and appeared to be dying from the cold. The question was what to do. The party had limited time to get over an 18,000-foot pass; they were battling the elements and altitude sickness. Every practical consideration told them to keep moving. That is what they did, after providing the Sadhu with some additional clothing and food. But they were continually troubled by the choice they made, and never knew if the Sadhu had lived or died. Had they sacrificed ethics for self-interest? Placed short-term goals above soul and spirit?

We selected the leadership gifts of authorship, love, power, and significance in part because they work: they produce better results and a more motivated and committed workforce. The practical question of what works is essential. Our skill and knowledge determine whether we get things right or wrong, make them better or worse. That theme is central to much of what we have written both before and since *Leading with Soul*. But as important as it is to know how to do things well, there is still the deeper question of what is worth doing. A spiritual path engages fundamental questions like those captured so well in the Rumi poem that opens the book: Where did I come from? What am I here to do? What is the meaning and purpose of my life? What is my destiny? In choosing to explore such questions and embark on a spiritual journey, we strengthen faith, deepen soul, and build spirit.

*When I think of words like **soul, spirit**, and **faith**, I generally associate them with theology and religious doctrine. Can leading with soul and taking a journey of spirit include secular perspectives and pursuits?*

It is true that books about spirituality often speak from a specific religious tradition, but that is not our purpose. The word *religion* implies a particular group of people bound by a vision of the divine expressed through shared beliefs, institutions, rituals, and artifacts. Every great religion offers special gifts, based on its unique spiritual tradition. Religion is often a path to spirituality, but it is not the only path.

Steve Camden recognizes from the beginning that it would be divisive and counterproductive to rely on a particular religion as a vehicle to introduce spirituality into his organization. In a multicultural world, organizations must make room for people of different faiths and no faith. The challenge that he and other leaders face is to find a language and create an inclusive conversation that speaks to people of many different perspectives. This is often challenging, as is illustrated in the many different ways people react to the simple word *God*. Some cannot imagine a conversation about spirituality without God at the center. Others recoil from the "G word." A few readers have told us they were disappointed that *Leading with Soul* did not put Jesus Christ at the center of its message. We want to speak to Christians, and we have learned from authors who have offered Christian interpretations of spirituality at work.[3] But ours is a diverse and inclusive caravan, and we invite spiritual seekers of all backgrounds and persuasions to join us in the search for faith, significance, and something bigger.

I liked the book, but did it change me? Was it supposed to?

Some readers tell us that the book changed them profoundly. Others feel let down, waiting for something dramatic that hasn't happened. The variety of individual responses convinces us that the reader, not the book, is the true author of change. Your responses to *Leading with Soul* are clues to understanding where you are on your own spiritual journey. For some readers, the book is a catalyst that starts them in a new direction. One wrote: "I am an engineer. Two plus two equals four; facts are facts. The other day my wife was engrossed in this book. When she left for the kitchen, I picked it up and started to read. Then it hit me right between the eyes: there's something missing in my life. I am now searching for something bigger."

For other readers, *Leading with Soul* has served as a guide or map for rekindling soul and spirit in relationships. Many individuals report discovering ways to make individual journeys less lonely and shared quests more fulfilling. More than one couple told us that their joint reading of the book opened a dialogue that strengthened or even saved their marriage.

For still others the book has confirmed a path they have been on for some time. As a reader from Iowa wrote: "I felt I was on the right track, but it sure felt awfully lonely and scary. With Steve and Maria as my companions, I gained new strength and courage to plow ahead." An art teacher wrote: "An instructor gave me a copy of *Leading with Soul* to read. I have no idea what this book has touched inside of me, but it feels good. As a 27-year-old African American male I feel lost in this society. Your book has challenged me to start where few of us do . . . with our souls."

A number of readers reported giving *Leading with Soul* to colleagues, friends, or loved ones, hoping it might serve others as it had them. Sometimes that gift has been inspired. An undergraduate wrote that his father gave him "a copy of the book to read. Initially, I wasn't really sure why. But after reading the book I figured it out. He wanted me to have the same kind of experience he had. I think it made him a better boss. But I know it's made him a really good dad."

Some individuals encounter the book when they are, like Jill in the final chapter, on the verge of a wakeup call from their soul—when questions of identity, faith, and direction beckon with growing urgency. The letter of one such reader, a Japanese manager, captures in a powerful and poignant way the feelings many others share in today's chaotic and confusing world:

Impressions of *Leading with Soul* Humbly Offered

Personal information: Employed in a management position with a large company. Forty-nine years of age.

My feelings these days:
Even though I have been taught that I shouldn't depend on things, I want to cling to something. Even though I have been taught that I shouldn't seek form either, I want something I can see. Even though I have been taught that work is not everything, I aim for constantly higher levels of performance.

I feel it is not right if I don't seek something and work my hardest at it. I have decided on goals for my work that I cannot attain, while suspecting that they are exaggerated or fanciful. Therefore, I am always tired.

I want a break.

However, if I'm not moving, with my eyes fixed firmly on the future, I feel that I will slip down from something. If I try to unburden myself and relax, I just become that much tenser. I want to feel good. Although it should be close at hand, right in front of my eyes, I don't have the energy to grasp it.

I don't have the courage to bare myself. If I bare myself, I am afraid that I will be looked down on and will lose something. Because I've felt that I was lacking, more than others, I've always set my sights higher. Now within the company organization, I feel I am on a level with others. I am a manager. I even have some people under me. I am a leader. But, now, I am tired and want to rest. Really.

I want to draw the picture that I want and converse with the beauty of nature.

What whimpering.

However, I do feel that I would like to put a little more life back into myself. This book, which came to my attention in my discontent, was forceful. I want to learn more.

I want to understand more deeply about spirituality. I am a forty-nine-year-old male, yearning to make himself shine. This book has warned me.

However, I don't know specifically what to do. I want to know. I want to talk about it with someone. These are my impressions. It would be wonderful if someone could enlighten me.

This letter illustrates the mixture of awareness, confusion, and yearning common in individuals who are on the threshold of a new level of spiritual exploration. The writer's reflection is filled with questions about the spiritual journey: What's really happening in my life? What am I missing? Where do I need to go from here? How do I get there? These are questions all of us face.

How Do I . . . ?

What is it that I keep missing on my journey?
What lesson do I not see?

The inner journey to discover one's spiritual core is never easy. As Maria told Steve, there is no road map. Along the way, signposts and clues provide direction. Yet often our attention is so riveted on where we are trying to go that we miss the small, often intangible signs that might lead us to our personal treasure store. An authentic journey is not literal but metaphoric, a discovery. As Maria tells Steve, it's not like a trip to Chicago—a straight-line trip to a known destination. Looking for concrete lessons misses the point.

If you're not learning, you may need to look harder and risk more. The journey will bring few lessons if you never leave home. A letter from Dan, a U.S. health care consultant, reveals an individual who is beginning to realize it's time for him to move beyond his comfort zone:

> I have a good job, live in a beautiful neighborhood, and own a wonderful home. I have a loving wife, and two terrific kids. The other day on the way to work, I realized that my heart is not into what I am doing. I sort of hit the wall, a real personal crisis. The next day I drove to Atlanta to talk to my best friend. He gave me a copy of *Leading with Soul*. I took it home with me and put it on the nightstand behind my bed. The next night I could not get to sleep. I picked up the book and took it to the living room. I read it from cover to cover. It was a very moving experience. I got up and walked through the darkened house. I realized how much I had

missed. I went back to the bedroom and woke up my wife. I said, "Honey, I have not been here for you and the kids. From now on things are going to be different." The next day I resigned my job. I'm not exactly sure what I will be doing. But a scary journey feels much better than a meaningless job and an empty life.

Even before he encountered *Leading with Soul,* Dan knew something was wrong. The book confirmed his dawning intuition that it was time to move in new directions. Because it came along at just the right time, it helped him to structure and deepen the quest he already knew, even if dimly, he had to undertake.

Where do I find a Maria—my own spiritual guide?

The simplest answer is look and you will probably find. An old Buddhist saying tells us, "When the pupil is ready, the teacher will appear." How does the pupil get ready? There is truth in the proverb "the Lord helps those who help themselves." But there is an equally important truth in the biblical injunction "they that wait upon the Lord shall renew their strength."[4] We need to be active in looking for a teacher, but we must also let go of the pride and defenses that cause us to insist that we can take care of ourselves and need no help from anyone else. Until we're ready to acknowledge our weakness, vulnerability, and incompleteness, we are not likely to find our own Maria.

Having accepted ourselves as we are, we still have to get out and look. "Ask, and it will be given you; seek, and you will find; knock, and it will be opened to you."[5] If you're not finding your own Maria where you've been looking, expand your options. Get involved in new activities or groups. Look for the right spiritual home. Sometimes that's as simple as searching out the right house of worship. Other times it might mean getting involved in community or charitable activities that deepen your growth and bring you into contact with new people. The key is to be both receptive and active. Take time to be with yourself and to pray or meditate. Make time as well to be with others to learn and grow. Open yourself to possibilities—life abounds with teachers and lessons.

We know there are many guides out there because so many readers have written to say they know a Maria. These guides have many different names, and they are remarkably diverse in age, profession, gender, and just about everything else. The challenge is finding someone who cares enough about you and your development to be willing to offer an optimal blend of love and challenge. Sometimes two people can do that for one another—as in some marriages.

How can we become more aware of the spiritual guides that come in and out of our lives and embrace them rather than put them off?

We need to listen to those small voices that call our attention to things outside our normal awareness. We also need to pay attention when day-to-day experiences—such as conversations at work, over a meal, or at a social event—trigger thoughts or images that might take us somewhere important if we follow where they lead. Stories, in particular, help us see intangible things we would otherwise miss. A business executive, Jackie Shrago, wrote to describe this insight that hit her in response to a story in the book:

> The story about a stream in Chapter Four struck a chord that described my own journey. The business that I co-founded had been my stream of life for ten years. It embodied the profession I had developed, all of my creative energy, my family, even my soul. And then, I sold my share of the business and signed a no-compete agreement. Suddenly, with my signature on those agree-

ments, just like the stream I arrived at a desert. I no longer knew who I was. I had lost all the ways in which I had defined myself. The wind called, but I didn't know how to give up who I had been. All were gone: my profession, my daily activities, my family. I had to identify anew the essence of my soul and give in to the wind and the desert to find myself on the other side. Gradually my technology experience, my early passion for teaching, and my political experience during the desert years emerged and blended together in a new stream to create new opportunities in the emerging field of the Internet. Five years later, there was again a stream flowing in my life, with direction and focus. Without giving in to the desert and the wind it would have been difficult if not impossible to imagine the new beginning, reclaim my soul, and identify the new stream of life. Thanks for helping me put words to my story and my journey.

How can I use Leading with Soul *to foster a dialogue with friends or coworkers?*

Readers have often asked how to break the ice and start discussing soul and spirit. There are many paths to a deeper conversation, and each group needs to find the route that works for it.

But here are a few possibilities that have worked for the authors or other readers:

Sometimes, it helps to begin by talking about someone else. For example, people who have read *Leading with Soul* can talk about their reactions to the story and the characters. What parts of the story do they like best? Which do they like least? How do they react to Steve? To Maria? Do they identify more with one or the other? What's bothering Steve when he first meets Maria? How does she respond? Is she helpful or not? Why, for example, does Maria tell Steve to get lost? Is that good advice or bad? What happens for Steve when he tries to follow it?

In talking about Steve and Maria, people naturally glide into reflecting on themselves as well. The differences in the ways individuals see the characters and the story are important and fruitful sources of learning, particularly when people avoid the temptation to defend their own interpretations and to foist them on others. If, for example, one person is drawn to Steve Camden but another sees him as weak and confused, the different perceptions probably say more about the two individuals than about the character in the book. Both of them might learn from a dialogue about their differing perceptions.

Look for ways to use expressive, or "soulful," media such as drama, poetry, music, and art. Some groups have focused on the poems in *Leading with Soul*. Ask people to choose the poem they like best. Individuals can read aloud the poems they have selected and talk about what the poems say. A comfortable room, candles, and music in the background can all add to the mood.

Showing segments of videos or feature films can be an avenue to powerful discussions. The better or more popular a film, the more likely it is to contain important messages about life, love, leadership, and the spiritual journey. This is true of box office sensations such as *Avatar, Titanic, The Lion King, The Godfather (I and II)*, and the original *Star Wars* trilogy. It's true of Oscar winners like *The King's Speech, Slumdog Millionaire, Million Dollar Baby,* and *Lord of the Rings,* as well as classics like *It's a Wonderful Life, To Kill a Mockingbird,* and *Citizen Kane.* Spiritual questions abound in any of Shakespeare's major plays, including *Hamlet, MacBeth,* and *Othello.* Powerful stories of leadership and soul can be found in films like *Gandhi, Schindler's List,* and *Mr. Smith Goes to Washington.*

Storytelling is a powerful medium. Individuals can compose stories about their life journey, focusing on the people, places, and events that have influenced their understanding of leadership. Groups can also tell stories about themselves and their situations, as they did in Steve Camden's organization at company gatherings.

The search for soul and meaning can be an individual or group endeavor. It can also be commissioned as a corporate-wide undertaking. Once Steve found his own inner core, he was able to help his organization find its spiritual center. His efforts at leadership were not always a success, but over time, he inspired his organization to reap its full potential. Across the world and economic sectors, other corporate-wide quests are helping to infuse work with soul.

As a middle manager I feel strangled. I feel I'm on a leash, and I get jerked back if I step out too far. How do I lead with soul when I don't feel it from above?

Most of us are in the middle in one way or another, which makes it easy to feel trapped. We feel the pressure to follow directives from above and to ensure that sometimes unwilling subordinates comply and get things done. It's easy to feel like a yo-yo— bouncing first one way then another, depending on who's pulling the string.

If your workplace or your boss is hopelessly toxic, ask whether hanging on is really your best option. Moving on is often the first step to spiritual development. But no workplace is perfect, and leading with soul offers a way out of feeling trapped. The less you're in touch with who you are, what you value, and what you believe, the more you're vulnerable to feeling lost and adrift, easily pushed this way and that by the pressures around you. But as you identify your spiritual center and learn to lead from your heart, you have a solid base from which you can influence up and inspire down. Granted, it's not risk free. Telling the truth and standing firm for what you believe won't always win friends. Sometimes people may question whether you're a team player.

But don't give in too easily to fear of being the nail that stands up and gets pounded. Too much fear and conformity are bad for organizations and individuals. Yes, you could annoy the boss or even get fired. That's scary in an era when almost everyone has friends who have struggled to find work. But the risks need to be balanced against the many examples of courage and integrity that have produced huge dividends in the long run. If you need to, you may well find a better job elsewhere. And you might even get promoted by your current employer. Either way you will feel better and more fulfilled. You may delight in the joy of making a difference, and your integrity will be intact. Not a bad legacy to pass on.

Kristen Ragusin, a financial consultant with one of America's biggest stockbrokers, elegantly illustrates the possibilities that are unleashed when a single individual finds ways to integrate spirituality with work. Asked if there wasn't a conflict between the bottom-line focus of her profession and her spirituality, she responded:

> I don't see life divided like that. My work is a continual voyage of self-discovery. There's nothing like money to reveal people's values and their sense of meaning. My engagement with clients brings up the deepest questions. Who am I? Who are these people? Often they come in scared, excited, happy, guilty, all at once. Then financial planning is itself a process of self-discovery— where are your priorities, what do you want to do in retirement? People are generally uncomfortable with knowing who they are other than as consumers of the American capitalist myth. I know that consumerism is filling a black hole inside, so I listen for the signs of that in their story. In them, I see the richness of who we all are, how our core issues are all the same.[6]

Ragusin understands that financial planning is about money, but she is wise enough to see that it's also about things even more important than money. "When a new client comes in, I simply hold the questions: Who is this soul? What does he or she cherish? That's where I go now, and the plan is simple then."[7]

She has also found that the clearer she has become about the spiritual dimension in her work, the easier the work itself has become and the more successful she has been.

I believe that leadership involves the giving of gifts, but I worry about how people will respond. Aren't there some tensions here?

In gift giving, as in most of the interesting things in life, there are dilemmas. Giving authorship creates opportunities for people to put their signature on their work but individual priorities can undermine an organization's standards. Consumers expect consistency in goods and services and become upset when their expectations are not met. Giving people power carries risks. There is always someone who will take advantage for personal gain. The gift of love extends caring and compassion, but what do you do when tough decisions need to be made that will affect people's lives and livelihoods? Trying to create an organization that infuses work with a deeply felt sense of significance flies in the face of today's widespread cynicism. People may interpret the gift of significance as another round of management manipulation. Steve Camden experienced firsthand many of these dilemmas, sometimes painfully. Maria's coaching helped, but the key was that he kept trying and learned from his mistakes.

It's important to recognize the risks and dilemmas because then we're less likely to be startled or discouraged if we trip over them occasionally. We'll fail for sure if our gifts are halfhearted or inauthentic. But as we continue our spiritual journey, we acquire new gifts and increase our capacity to give to others. As we deepen our own faith, we understand even more deeply that we need to offer our gifts to others for their sake as well as our own.

How do you lead difficult employees?

Leadership would be easier if everyone around us was cooperative, upbeat, and a joy to work with. But most workplaces contain at least a few people who seem close to impossible. When we encounter difficult people, we may assume that the problem is them. But it's often the case that people who seem difficult are having problems with their work situation. Instead of blaming people, it's more productive to ask what factors in their environment may be causing them problems. That's where leadership gifts can help. Sometimes, difficult people don't believe anyone really cares about them, and they may not realize their actions are what keep people at a distance. In such cases even a modest dose of caring and compassion can make a surprising difference.

Other times, people feel no sense of real accomplishment, of seeing how their efforts produce something they can be proud of. Many progressive employers have found that giving more opportunities for authorship can transform complainers into engaged workers. We've all heard that power corrupts, but powerlessness is even more corrosive. People who feel powerless are almost always pains in the butt to those with power. Sharing power goes a long way toward letting people know that they can have some clout in making a better work environment. People are also likely to become difficult when they feel their life and work have no real meaning. That's where the gift of significance can work magic. Even the most disgruntled employee can sign on to accomplish something that makes sense, or can get caught up in the spirit of authentic ritual, ceremony, or stories. So the next time you find yourself labeling someone as difficult, look around you or look in the mirror for the root cause.

Has fact-driven, scientifically oriented, rigorous education created a cohort of students who simply cannot comprehend or relate to the language of soul and spirit?
Scratch and sniff beneath their self-assured and rational veneers, and you find that many of today's students are searching for deeper, more fulfilling, and more meaningful lives. A recent

study found that college students become more interested in spiritual questions even though colleges rarely use some of the most powerful means for fostering spiritual development, such as meditation and self-reflection. Students' journeys are often taken alone and rarely shared because many young people think they need to mask this personal search from others. When they're given the opportunity to drop their masks and share their inner thoughts, pains, and passions with others, they relish the connection.

But where do they typically get the chance? Rarely in class-rooms. Sometimes in enlightened companies. Most often in more informal settings—sororities and fraternities, sports teams, or even gangs. Good education needs to balance mind and soul, head and heart. A classroom is a great place to launch a student's quest for a more fulfilling life.

Spreading Spirit

Given the increasing use of temporary workers to reduce costs and increase flexibility, how can spirited leaders draw these short-termers into the fold?

Part of the answer here is to be bone-honest about the nature of the relationship. It may not be a long-term marriage, but it can be a mutually rewarding short-term love affair. Robert

Waterman has characterized the modern employee-employer relationship as one in which the boss promises a fair wage, a rewarding job, the best training available, and respect. The employee reciprocates with hard work, high commitment, and temporary loyalty. When the relationship is terminated, it is ideally done with caring, compassion, and assurance that the employee will land a job someplace else and that the employer will not have to worry about client poaching or trading of competitive secrets.[8] In a context of economic turmoil, reality often falls short of that ideal.

Tracy Kidder has described how both workers and bosses poured heart and soul into the development of a new computer. At the end the individuals went their separate ways, but they carried with them pride in accomplishing a difficult task and the promise of relationships that would last a lifetime. As Dan West, one of the group's leaders, commented: "It was a summer romance. But that's all right. Summer romances are some of the best things that ever happen."[9]

How do educational leaders help teachers become believers in their potential and their capacity to change?

We have all heard from teachers and school administrators how hard it is to keep the faith in the face of almost overwhelming challenges and lukewarm public support. Too often teachers are told that test scores are the only important measure of their effectiveness, and the content they transmit is far more important than who they are. But most of us have had a teacher somewhere along the line who made a profound and positive difference. We may or may not remember much of the information that teachers passed along, but we remember a caring human being who chose to invest in our learning. As Tracy Kidder has observed:

> Teachers usually have no way of knowing that they have made a difference in a child's life, even when they have made a dramatic one. But for children who are used to thinking of themselves as stupid or not worth talking to or deserving rape and beatings, a good teacher can provide an astonishing revelation. A good teacher can give a child at least a chance to feel "She thinks I'm worth something, maybe I am." Good teachers put snags in the river of children passing by, and over the years, they redirect hundreds of lives. Many people find it easy to imagine unseen webs of malevolent conspiracy in the world, and they are not always

wrong. But there is also an innocence that conspires to hold humanity together, and it is made up of people who can never fully know the good they have done.[10]

Leaders can help teachers acknowledge and appreciate the good that they do. Indeed, this is an issue not just for teachers but also for many other workers who wonder if they are getting anything done or if their work really makes a difference. These are essentially problems of significance. The challenge for leaders is to go beyond a focus on day-to-day management concerns and crises and to focus on the larger purpose of work and of the institution in which the work is carried out. Budgets have to be balanced and paper has to be pushed, but that's the easy part of being a manager or a schoolteacher. The deeper and more important task is to give passionate, relentless attention to mission and purpose, continually seeking ways to offer the gift of significance to one's constituents.

Are you yourselves currently involved in spirituality programs?

We do seminars and workshops that feature ideas drawn from this book, but we're only a small part of a much larger movement. Many individuals and organizations are engaged in activities designed to bring soul and spirit into work. The Robert K. Greenleaf Center in Indianapolis has an active program on servant leadership that takes seriously the spiritual dimension in organizations. A growing number of conferences and workshops explore issues of spirituality at work. Many organizations are developing their own internal programs to explore the spiritual dimension. Prince Philipp of Liechtenstein, chairman of Liechtenstein Global Trust, created a leadership academy for his international group of financial managers. For three weeks, participants created art, took aikido lessons, learned to juggle, and took part in a rich set of expressive experiences. Prince Philipp told us, "I already have very good managers. But in today's world our company needs really good leaders. To lead, you've got to be in touch with your heart and soul." We believe that the business world will see more programs like this in the future.

Have you thought about pulling together a group of people to share stories about their personal journeys and experiences at work?

Yes, and so have many others. Since *Leading with Soul* was published, we have convened occasions for people to share stories about their personal journeys or about the joys and trials, the ups and downs of life at work. The energy, humor, and poignancy such events draw forth offer us constant delight. It has been said that God created humans because he loves stories. Our experiences show that it's true.

NOTES

Prelude: In Search of Soul and Spirit

1. Virgil H. Adams III, C. R. Snyder, Kevin L. Rand, Elisa Ann O'Donnell, David R. Sigmon, and Kim M. Pulvers, "Hope in the Workplace," in Robert A. Giacalone and Carole L. Jurkiewicz, *Handbook of Workplace Spirituality and Organizational Performance* (Armonk, N.Y.: Sharpe, 2010).

2. In the Gospel According to St. Mark (8:36, King James Version), for example, Mark tells us that Jesus asked, "For what shall it profit a man, if he shall gain the whole world, and lose his own soul." See also Matthew 16:26 and Luke 9:25.

3. M. Fox, *The Reinvention of Work: A New Vision of Livelihood for Our Time* (San Francisco: Harper San Francisco, 1994), pp. 1–2.

4. Compare J. Hillman, *A Blue Fire: Selected Writings,* edited by T. Moore (New York: HarperCollins, 1991), p. 113.

5. W. Whitman, "Passage to India," in M. Van Doren (ed.), *The Portable Walt Whitman* (New York: Penguin, 1977), p. 284.

Interlude 1: Reclaiming Your Soul

1. J. Campbell, *A Joseph Campbell Companion: Reflections on the Art of Living,* edited by D. K. Osbon (New York: HarperPerennial, 1995), p. 24.

2. A. Schweitzer, quoted in P. L. Berman, *The Search for Meaning: Americans Talk About What They Believe and Why* (New York: Ballantine, 1990), p. vi.

3. R. D. Putnam, "Bowling Alone: America's Declining Social Capital," *Journal of Democracy* 6 (1995): 67–78.

4. R. E. Lane, *The Loss of Happiness in Market Democracies* (New Haven, Conn.: Yale University Press, 2000).

5. J. C. Collins and J. I. Porras, *Built to Last: Successful Habits of Visionary Companies* (New York: HarperBusiness, 1994).

6. S. Reynolds, *Thoughts from Chairman Buffett: Thirty Years of Unconventional Wisdom from the Sage of Omaha* (New York: HarperBusiness, 1998), p. 37.

7. 1 John 2:27, as rendered by S. Mitchell (ed.), *The Enlightened Mind: An Anthology of Sacred Prose* (New York: HarperCollins, 1991), p. 32.

8. Mitchell, *The Enlightened Mind,* p. 209. The novice was Hui-Hai, who became a Zen master himself. In telling this story, Hui-Hai added, "From that day on, I stopped looking elsewhere. All you have to do is look into your own mind; then the marvelous reality will manifest itself at all times" (p. 56).

9. I. I. Mitroff and E. A. Denton, *A Spiritual Audit of Corporate America* (San Francisco: Jossey-Bass, 1999), pp. xv–xvi. Emphasis added.

10. C. A. Hammerschlag, *The Theft of the Spirit* (New York: Simon & Schuster, 1993), pp. 170–171.

11. E. Kurtz and K. Ketcham, *The Spirituality of Imperfection: Modern Wisdom from Classic Stories* (New York: Bantam, 1992), p. 35.

12. D. Whyte, *The Heart Aroused: Poetry and the Preservation of the Soul in Corporate America* (New York: Doubleday/Currency, 1994).

13. Campbell, *A Joseph Campbell Companion,* p. 24.

Interlude 2: Leaning Into Your Fear

1. Lao Tzu, quoted in S. Mitchell (ed.), *The Enlightened Heart: An Anthology of Sacred Poetry* (New York: HarperCollins, 1989), p. 16.

2. A. Ulanov and B. Ulanov, *Primary Speech: A Psychology of Prayer* (Louisville, Ky.: Westminster John Knox Press, 1982), p. vii.

3. E. Klein and J. B. Izzo, *Awakening Corporate Soul: Four Paths to Unleash the Power of People at Work* (Lions Bay, B.C., Canada: Fairwinds Press, 1999).

4. Seng-Ts'an, "The Mind of Absolute Trust," quoted in Mitchell, *The Enlightened Heart,* p. 27. Seng-Ts'an (?–606) was a Zen Master.

5. William Blake, quoted in Mitchell, *The Enlightened Heart,* p. 95.

6. C. A. Hammerschlag, *The Theft of the Spirit* (New York: Simon & Schuster, 1992), p. 50.

7. B. Irwin, quoted in Hammerschlag, *The Theft of the Spirit,* p. 45.

8. Hammerschlag, *The Theft of the Spirit,* p. 45.

9. E. Kurtz and K. Ketcham, *The Spirituality of Imperfection: Modern Wisdom from Classic Stories* (New York: Bantam, 1992), p. 47.

10. E. Becker, *The Denial of Death* (New York: Free Press, 1975), p. 34.

11. Kurtz and Ketcham, *The Spirituality of Imperfection,* p. 56.

12. J. Campbell, *The Power of Myth* (New York: Doubleday, 1988), p. 5.

Interlude 3: Community and the Cycle of Giving

1. Rumi, quoted in A. Harvey (ed.), *Speaking Flame: Rumi* (Ithaca, N.Y.: Meeramma, 1989), p. 86.

2. C. Pearson, *Awakening the Heroes Within* (San Francisco: Harper San Francisco, 1991), p. 1.

3. K. Gibran, *The Prophet* (New York: Knopf, 1970), pp. 32–33.

4. D. Chatterjee, *Leading Consciously: A Pilgrimage Toward Self-Mastery* (Boston: Butterworth-Heinemann, 1998), p. 150.

5. A. Delios, "How Can Organizations Be Competitive but Dare to Care?" *Academy of Management Perspectives* 24, no. 3 (2010): 25–36.

6. J. Pfeffer, "Building Sustainable Organizations: The Human Factor," *Academy of Management Perspectives* 24, no. 1 (2010): 34–45.

7. B. Burlingham, *Small Giants: Companies That Choose to Be Great Instead of Big* (New York: Portfolio, 2005).

8. Burlingham, *Small Giants*.

9. C. Whitmyer (ed.), *In the Company of Others* (New York: Putnam, 1993), p. 81.

10. T. Moore, *Care of the Soul: A Guide for Cultivating Depth and Sacredness in Everyday Life* (New York: HarperCollins, 1991), p. 77.

11. Guiraut de Bornelh, quoted in J. Campbell, *A Joseph Campbell Companion: Reflections on the Art of Living,* edited by D. K. Osbon (New York: HarperPerennial, 1995), p. 77.

12. J. R. Hackman, G. R. Oldham, R. Janson, and K. Purdy, "A New Strategy for Job Enrichment," in L. E. Boone and D. D. Bowen (eds.), *The Great Writings in Management and Organizational Behavior* (New York: Random House, 1987), p. 315.

13. We discuss these and other sources of power in more detail in chapter nine of L. G. Bolman and T. E. Deal, *Reframing Organizations: Artistry, Choice, and Leadership* (San Francisco: Jossey-Bass, 2008).

14. T. Bjørgo (ed.), *Root Causes of Terrorism: Myths, Reality and Ways Forward* (New York: Routledge, 2005).

15. Bjørgo, *Root Causes of Terrorism*.

16. M. S. Peck, *The Different Drum: Community Making and Peace* (New York: Simon & Schuster, 1987), p. 71.

17. *Harvard Business Review,* "Howard Schultz on Starbucks' Turnaround." HBR Ideacast, June 24, 2010, http://blogs.hbr.org/ideacast/2010/06/howard-schultz-on-starbucks-tu.html.

18. D. Campbell, "If I'm in Charge, Why Is Everyone Laughing?" paper presented at the Center for Creative Leadership, Greensboro, N.C., 1983.

19. E. Griffin, *The Reflective Executive: A Spirituality of Business and Enterprise* (New York: Crossroad, 1993), p. 159.

20. Moore, *Care of the Soul,* p. 225.

21. C. P. Estés, *The Gift of Story* (New York: Ballantine, 1993), pp. 28–29.

22. Estés, *The Gift of Story,* pp. 28–29.

23. C. Arena, *Cause for Success: 10 Companies That Put Profits Second and Came in First* (Novato, Calif.: New World Library, 2004).

24. B. Googins, P. H. Mirvis, and S. A. Rochlin, *Beyond Good Company: Next Generation Corporate Citizenship* (New York: Palgrave Macmillan, 2007), p. 45.

25. Googins, Mirvis, and Rochlin, *Beyond Good Company,* p. 18.

26. Googins, Mirvis, and Rochlin, *Beyond Good Company,* p. 19.

27. Googins, Mirvis, and Rochlin, *Beyond Good Company,* p. 19.

28. Googins, Mirvis, and Rochlin, *Beyond Good Company,* p. 19.

Interlude 4: Expressing the Spirit

1. Cited in S. Mitchell (ed.), *The Enlightened Mind: An Anthology of Sacred Prose* (New York: HarperCollins, 1991), p. 191.

2. Kushner, quoted in P. Berman, *The Courage of Conviction* (New York: Ballantine, 1985), p. 164.

3. J. Campbell, *The Power of Myth* (New York: Doubleday, 1988), p. 48.

4. B. Lopez, *Crow and Weasel* (New York: Farrar, Straus & Giroux, 1998).

5. J. James, "African Philosophy, Theory, and Living Thinkers," in J. James and R. Farmer (eds.), *Spirit, Space, and Survival: African American Women in (White) Academe* (New York: Routledge, 1993), p. 31.

6. S. K. Langer, *Philosophy in a New Key* (Cambridge, Mass.: Harvard University Press, 1951), p. xvii.

7. Liszt, cited in Langer, *Philosophy in a New Key,* p. 236.

8. Louis V. Gerstner. *Who Says Elephants Can't Dance? Inside IBM's Historic Turnaround* (New York: HarperCollins, 2002), p. 182.

9. See Jeffrey Pfeffer, "Business and the Spirit: Management Practices That Sustain Values," in R. A. Giacalone and C. L. Jurkiewicz, *Handbook of Workplace Spirituality and Organizational Performance* (Armonk, N.Y.: Sharpe, 2010).

10. H. Cox, *The Feast of Fools* (Cambridge, Mass.: Harvard University Press, 1969), p. 12.

Chapter Sixteen: The Twilight of Leadership

1. Dante Alighieri, *The Divine Comedy: Purgatory,* canto 27, translated by S. T. Massey, in "The Act of Creation and the Process of Learning," keynote address presented at the Cultural Congress, Indianapolis, Ind., March 12, 1994.

Chapter Seventeen: Deep Refuge

1. Rumi, "Why Organize a Universe This Way?" in J. Moyne and C. Barks, *Open Secret: Versions of Rumi* (Putney, Vt.: Threshold Books, 1984), p. 79.

Interlude 5: The Cycle of the Spirit

1. Epigraph: A. E. Housman, "Wake: The Silver Dust Returning," in *A Shropshire Lad* (London: Paul, Trench, Treubner, 1896).

2. S. B. Nuland, *How We Die* (New York: Knopf, 1994).

3. E. Becker, *The Denial of Death* (New York: Free Press, 1973), p. 27.

4. E. Kurtz and K. Ketcham, *The Spirituality of Imperfection: Modern Wisdom from Classic Stories* (New York: Bantam, 1992), p. 58.

5. N. Frye, *Myth and Metaphor: Selected Essays, 1974–1988,* edited by R. D. Denham (Charlottesville: University Press of Virginia, 1990), p. 224.

6. May, Ory, and Myten, p. 294.

7. P. Coelho, *The Alchemist* (San Francisco: Harper San Francisco, 1993), p. 167.

8. Becker, *The Denial of Death,* p. 285.

9. A. Greeley, quoted in in P. Berman, *The Courage of Conviction* (New York: Ballantine, 1985), pp. 114–115.

10. S. Kierkegaard, quoted in Becker, *The Denial of Death,* pp. 257–258.

11. Coelho, *The Alchemist,* p. 167.

12. G. de Purucker, *Wind of the Spirit* (Pasadena, Calif.: Theosophical University Press, 1984), p. 17.

Postlude: Soul at Work

1. B. Burlingham, *Small Giants: Companies That Choose to Be Great Instead of Big* (New York: Portfolio, 2005).

2. Burlingham, *Small Giants.*

3. Burlingham, *Small Giants.*

4. D. Stafford, "Energy, Emotion Aid Auto Plant," *Kansas City Star,* February 9, 2000, pp. C-1 and C-4.

5. J. Condon, D. Dee, and F. Noyes, personal communications, September 2000.

6. T. Gunning, "I Have No Choice: An Interview with Tex Gunning," *EnlightenNext Magazine,* March-May 2005. Online at www.enlightennext.org/magazine/j28/gunning.asp.

7. B. K. Googins, P. H. Mirvis, and S. A. Rochlin, *Beyond Good Company: Next Generation Corporate Citizenship* (New York: Palgrave/Macmillan), pp. 53–54.

8. Googins, Mirvis, and Rochlin, *Beyond Good Company,* p. 54.

9. P. Hawken, *The Ecology of Commerce: A Declaration of Sustainability* (New York: HarperBusiness, 1994).

10. R. Anderson, "Corporate Balancing Act: How Businesses Can Bolster Profits While Protecting the Environment," *Washington Post,* January 28, 2010. Online at http://voices.washingtonpost.com/shortstack/2010/01/corporate_balancing_act_how_bu.html; accessed February 14, 2011.

11. C. Arena, *Cause for Success: 10 Companies That Put Profits Second and Came in First* (Novato, Calif.: New World Library, 2004).

12. P. Levering and M. Moskowitz, *The 100 Best Companies to Work for in America* (New York: Plume, 1994), p. 138.

13. M. Benefiel, *Soul at Work: Spiritual Leadership in Organizations* (New York: Seabury, 2005), p. 24.

14. Benefiel, *Soul at Work,* p. 24

15. M. Lewis, "Chef Executive," *Small Business Chicago,* November 2003. Online at www.sbnonline.com/Local/Article/5459/68/0/Chef_executive.aspx; accessed February 14, 2011.

16. K. Reagan, "Industry with Heart: The Pampered Chef," *Direct Selling News.com,* June 2008. Available online at http://test.directsellingnews.com/index.php/entries_archive_display/the_pampered_chef.

17. J. Stack, *The Great Game of Business* (New York: Currency/Doubleday, 1994). Basic information about the approach and links to additional resources are available online at www.greatgame.com.

18. K. Killian, F. Perez, and C. Siehl, "Ricardo Semler and Semco, S.A." Glendale, Az.: Thunderbird, the American Graduate School of International Management, 1998; R. Semler, *Maverick: The Success Story Behind the World's Most Unusual Workplace* (New York: Warner Books, 1993).

19. Ricardo Semler, cited in Killian, Perez, and Siehl, 1998, p. 2.

20. Googins, Mirvis, and Rochlin, *Beyond Good Company.*

21. Googins, Mirvis, and Rochlin, *Beyond Good Company,* p. 119.

22. Googins, Mirvis, and Rochlin, *Beyond Good Company,* p. 119.

23. Debashis Chatterjee, *Leading Consciously: A Pilgrimage Toward Self-Mastery* (Boston: Butterworth-Heinemann, 1998).

24. Arena, *Cause for Success*, p. 51.

25. David Batstone, *Saving the Corporate Soul—and (Who Knows?) Maybe Your Own* (San Francisco: Jossey-Bass, 2003), pp. 243–244.

Continuing a Spirited Dialogue

1. S. Trott, *The Holy Man* (New York: Riverhead, 1995).

2. B. McCoy, "The Parable of the Sadhu," *Harvard Business Review*, September-October 1983, p. 103.

3. Examples of works that bring a Christian perspective include L. B. Jones, *Jesus, CEO: Using Ancient Wisdom for Visionary Leadership* (New York: Hyperion, 1996); R. Marshall, *God@Work* (Racine, Wisc.: Treasures Media, 2006); G. F. Pierce, *Spirituality at Work: 10 Ways to Balance Your Life on the Job* (Chicago: Loyola, 2005); M. L. Russell, *Our Souls at Work* (Boise, Idaho: Russell Media, 2010).

4. Isaiah 40:31, King James Bible.

5. Matthew 7:7, Bible, New International Version 1984.

6. Kristen Ragusin, quoted in R. Housden, *Sacred America: The Emerging Spirit of the People* (New York: Simon & Schuster, 1999), pp. 55–56.

7. Ragusin in Housden, p. 58.

8. R. H. Waterman, *What America Does Best: Learning from Companies That Put People First* (New York: Norton, 1994).

9. T. Kidder, *Soul of a New Machine* (Boston: Back Bay Books, 2000), p. 287.

10. T. Kidder, *Among Schoolchildren* (New York: HarperCollins, 1990), p. 313.

RECOMMENDED READINGS

Al-Suhrawardy, A.S.A. *The Sayings of Muhammad*. Boston: Tuttle, 1992.

Armstrong, K. *A History of God*. New York: Knopf, 1993.

Armstrong, K. *The Case for God*. New York: Anchor, 2010.

Autry, J. A. *Love and Profit: The Art of Caring Leadership*. New York: Morrow, 1991.

Batstone, David. *Saving the Corporate Soul*. San Francisco: Jossey-Bass, 2003.

Benefiel, M. *Soul at Work: Spiritual Leadership in Organizations*. New York: Seabury, 2005.

Benefiel, M. *The Soul of a Leader: Finding Your Path to Success and Fulfillment*. New York: Crossroad, 2008.

Berman, P. L. *The Courage of Conviction*. New York: Ballantine, 1985.

Berman, P. L. *The Search for Meaning: Americans Talk About What They Believe and Why*. New York: Ballantine, 1990.

Bolman, L. G., and Deal, T. E. *Reframing Organizations: Artistry, Choice, and Leadership*. San Francisco: Jossey-Bass, 1991.

Brown, J. "The Corporation as Community." In C. Whitmyer, *In the Company of Others*. New York: Putnam, 1993, pp. 130–137.

Campbell, J. *Hero with a Thousand Faces*. New York: World, 1956.

Campbell, J. *The Power of Myth*. New York: Doubleday, 1988.

Chittick, W. C. *The Sufi Path of Love: The Spiritual Teachings of Rumi*. Albany: State University of New York Press, 1983.

Coelho, P. *The Alchemist*. San Francisco: Harper San Francisco, 1993.

Collins, J. C., and Porras, J. I. *Built to Last: Successful Habits of Visionary Companies*. New York: HarperBusiness, 1994.

Cox, H. *The Feast of Fools*. Cambridge, Mass.: Harvard University Press, 1969.

Cox, H. *The Future of Faith*. New York: HarperCollins, 2009.

Delbecq, A. "Nourishing the Soul of the Leader: Inner Growth Matters." In J. V., Gallos, *Business Leadership*. San Francisco: Jossey-Bass: 2008.

Estés, C. P. *The Gift of Story*. New York: Ballantine, 1993.

Fox, M. *The Reinvention of Work: A New Vision of Livelihood for Our Time*. San Francisco: Harper San Francisco, 1994.

Giacalone, R. A., and Jurkiewicz, C. L. *Handbook of Workplace Spirituality and Organizational Performance*, 2nd ed. Armonk, N.Y.: Sharpe, 2010.

Giles, L. (ed.). *Musings of a Chinese Mystic: Selections from the Philosophy of Chuang Tzu*. London: John Murray, 1906.

Googins, B. K., Mirvis, P. H., and Rochlin, S. A. *Beyond Good Company: Next Generation Corporate Citizenship*. New York: Palgrave Macmillan, 2007.

Greenleaf, R. "The Leader as Servant." In C. Whitmyer, *In the Company of Others*. New York: Putnam, 1993.

Griffin, E. *The Reflective Executive: A Spirituality of Business and Enterprise*. New York: Crossroad, 1993.

RECOMMENDED READINGS

Hackman, J. R., Oldham, G. R., Janson, R., and Purdy, K. "A New Strategy for Job Enrichment." In L. E. Boone and D. D. Bowen, *The Great Writings in Management and Organizational Behavior.* New York: Random House, 1987.

Hammerschlag, C. A. *The Theft of the Spirit.* New York: Simon & Schuster, 1993.

Harvey, A. *Speaking Flame: Rumi.* Ithaca, N.Y.: Meeramma, 1989.

Harvey, A. *The Way of Passion: A Celebration of Rumi.* Berkeley, Calif.: Frog, 1994.

Hawley, J. *Reawakening the Spirit in Work: The Power of Dharmic Management.* San Francisco: Berrett-Koehler, 1993.

Heider, J. *The Tao of Leadership: Leadership Strategies for a New Age.* New York: Bantam, 1986.

Izutsu, T. *Sufism and Taoism: A Comparative Study of Key Philosophical Concepts.* Berkeley: University of California Press, 1983.

James, J. "African Philosophy, Theory, and Living Thinkers." In J. James and R. Farmer (eds.), *Spirit, Space and Survival: African American Women in (White) Academe.* New York: Routledge, 1993.

Kipnis, A. R. *Knights Without Armor.* New York: Tarcher/Perigee, 1991.

Klein, E., and Izzo, J. B. *Awakening Corporate Soul: Four Paths to Unleash the Power of People at Work.* Leucadia, Calif.: Fairwinds Press, 1995.

Kurtz, E., and Ketcham, K. *The Spirituality of Imperfection: Modern Wisdom from Classic Stories.* New York: Bantam, 1992.

Kushner, H. *Who Needs God.* New York: Summit, 1989.

Lane, R. E. *The Loss of Happiness in Market Democracies.* New Haven, Conn.: Yale University Press, 2000.

Langer, S. K. *Philosophy in a New Key*. Cambridge, Mass.: Harvard University Press, 1951.

May, R. *The Cry for Myth*. New York: Dell, 1991.

Mirvis, P. H. "Soul Work in Organizations." *Organization Science*, 1997, 8, 193–206.

Mitchell, S. (ed.). *The Enlightened Heart: An Anthology of Sacred Poetry*. New York: HarperCollins, 1989.

Mitchell, S. (ed.). *The Enlightened Mind: An Anthology of Sacred Prose*. New York: HarperCollins, 1991.

Mitroff, I. I., and Denton, E. A. *A Spiritual Audit of Corporate America*. San Francisco: Jossey-Bass: 1999.

Moore, T. (ed.). *A Blue Fire: Selected Writings by James Hillman*. New York: HarperCollins, 1991.

Moore, T. *Care of the Soul: A Guide for Cultivating Depth and Sacredness in Everyday Life*. New York: HarperCollins, 1991.

Moyne, J., and Barks, C. *Open Secret: Versions of Rumi*. Putney, Vt.: Threshold Books, 1984.

Needleman, J. *Money and the Meaning of Life*. New York: Doubleday, 1991.

Nuland, S. B. *How We Die*. New York: Knopf, 1994.

Pearson, C. *Awakening the Heroes Within*. San Francisco: Harper San Francisco, 1991.

Peck, M. S. "The Fallacy of Rugged Individualism." In C. Whitmyer, *In the Company of Others*. New York: Putnam, 1993, pp. 12–15.

Purucker, G. de. *Wind of the Spirit*. Pasadena, Calif.: Theosophical University Press, 1984.

Putnam, R. D. "Bowling Alone: America's Declining Social Capital." *Journal of Democracy*, 1995, 6, 67–78.

Shah, I. *Tales of the Dervishes*. New York: Dutton, 1969.

Starhawk. "Celebration: The Spirit of Community." In C. Whitmyer, *In the Company of Others*. New York: Putnam, 1993, pp. 93–100.

Trott, S. *The Holy Man*. New York: Riverhead, 1995.

Vigliaturo, C. M. "The Spirit of Work: Discovering Meaning in the Everyday." Unpublished master's thesis, Baker University, 1999.

Watts, A. W. *The Spirit of Zen: A Way of Life, Work and Art in the Far East*. Boston: Tuttle, 1992.

Whitmyer, C. *In the Company of Others*. New York: Putnam, 1993.

Whyte, D. *The Heart Aroused: Poetry and the Preservation of the Soul in Corporate America*. New York: Doubleday/Currency, 1994.

ACKNOWLEDGMENTS

From our first encounter to our production of this revised edition of *Leading with Soul*, our mutual journey has been more a series of serendipitous twists of fate than a simple, linear path. It began over thirty years ago when the two of us were paired to teach a course at the Harvard Graduate School of Education. We were mismatched—a Yale-schooled psychologist team-teaching with a Stanford-trained sociologist. Intellectual competition and combat prevailed in the early going, but we eventually found ways to combine our diverse perspectives and to create a multileveled perspective on organizations—the four frames that we describe in *Reframing Organizations*.

That early exploration into the cognitive side of leadership was deepened over a conversation at lunch with our friends at Jossey-Bass. As we describe in the book, we left that gathering committed to writing a book on the human spirit. It was not a direction either of us had anticipated. Once embarked we found it both more difficult and more rewarding than we had imagined. We spent countless hours exploring unfamiliar literary terrain and experimenting with new ways to write. We reached deeply into our individual and shared spiritual lives. Our journey continues to deepen our understanding of life's most important treasures. We hope this new edition will encourage others to reach out and explore life's mystery and magic, to touch with awe the depths of soul and the peaks of spirit, and to see life as a gift and leadership as a process of giving from one's heart.

In our journey together we have received advice, counsel, ideas, encouragement, and inspiration from literally thousands of people. Limits of space and memory prevent us from naming them all, but we're very aware of the magnitude of our debt to all who helped us persist and learn. We couldn't have done it by ourselves.

We want to thank our friends at Jossey-Bass. Lynn Luckow, Bill Hicks, Cedric Crocker, Kathy Vian, Lisa Shannon, Terry Armstrong Welch, and Lasell Whipple all made significant contributions to the first edition. Our long-time editor, Kathe Sweeney, and her talented team, including Mary Garrett, Dani Scoville, and Kristen Wiersma, have provided indispensable support and assistance on this new edition. We were blessed to work with Jeff Leeson, a very insightful and talented editorial partner who contributed in more ways than we can acknowledge to the quality of this edition. We were also fortunate to benefit again from the superb copyediting skills of Hilary Powers. The finished book is our progeny, but their assistance in a difficult delivery was invaluable.

We also continue to be grateful to a number of friends and colleagues who helped us with previous editions. They include Pam Hawkins, Robert Crowson, Tom Johnson, Linda Corey, Donna Culver, Linda French, Rich Davis, Mark Kriger, Bowen White, Susan Sonnenday Vogel, Lovett Weems, John Weston, Joseph Hough, Cheryl Lison, Gerry Di Nardo, Brad Bates, Teddy Bart, Casey Baylas, Brad Gray, and the late Edward Smith.

We also want to thank the many who have contributed to the development of this edition. We are grateful to all the readers who wrote to ask questions, share experiences and ideas, and encourage us. Cliff Baden, Margaret Benefiel, Sharon Blevins, Ellen Castro, Jim Clawson, John Jacobson, Bob Marx, Phil Mirvis, Judy Neal, Lee Robbins, and Peter Vaill are among the colleagues who share a deep commitment to understanding spirit at work and have helped us in important ways. We are particularly grateful to the late Peter Frost for his encouragement.

Lee is grateful to his colleagues at the Bloch School of Business and Public Administration at the University of Missouri-Kansas City, and offers particular thanks to Nancy Day, Doranne Hudson,

David Renz, and Marilyn Taylor. He's also grateful for invaluable support from Sandy Bretz and Bruce Kay. And he continues to appreciate the personal and spiritual sustenance of all the members of the Brookline Group: Dave Brown, Tim Hall, Todd Jick, Bill Kahn, Phil Mirvis, and Barry Oshry.

Terry's move from Vanderbilt to the University of Southern California's Rossier School added new colleagues: Gib Hentschke, Stu Gothold, and Carl Cohn. Warren Bennis at USC's Marshall School continues to be a wise mentor and valued friend.

Joan Vydra, a retired Illinois school principal, deepened our appreciation for stories and videos. Joe Condon, Dorinda Dee, and Frank Noyes (all formerly of the Lawndale Elementary School District) provided an excellent example of how leading with soul can pay off. The district's new superintendent, Ellen Dougherty, picks up the story where they left off.

Homa Aminmadani, who served Terry faithfully while he was on the road, now spends as much time as possible in the Netherlands with her grandchildren. Her continued friendship is deeply appreciated.

All our children have contributed to our joint and individual spiritual journeys. Janie Deal, now a chef in Twin Falls, Idaho, exemplifies in her career the kind of spunk and creativity we are writing about. Lee's children—Edward, Shelley, Lori, Scott,

ACKNOWLEDGMENTS

Christopher, and Bradley—and grandchildren—James, Jazmyne, and Foster—have all enriched his life and contributed to his learning.

Sandy Deal and Joan Gallos continue to play an integral role in our writing and our lives. As always, Joan and Sandy provided an environment of love and support, leavened with appropriate doses of probing questions and well-deserved criticism, that made it possible and worthwhile for us to keep going. Joan's generous comments and suggestions on the manuscript were invaluable.

Our search for traditional sources of spiritual wisdom has brought a new appreciation for all that our parents did to make us and our work possible. Florence and Eldred Bolman and Robert and Dorothy Deal helped us early in our lives to develop an appreciation for the world of spirit. Though it may have taken longer than they hoped for the fruits of their labor to mature, their influence is evident throughout this work.

THE AUTHORS

Lee G. Bolman is an author, teacher, and consultant. His earlier work on organizational leadership awakened his interest in the spiritual underpinnings of life at work. Born in Brooklyn, New York, to Midwestern parents, he has journeyed physically and spiritually between East and West ever since. Along the way, he earned a B.A. degree in history and a Ph.D. degree in organizational behavior at Yale University. He currently holds the Marion Bloch/Missouri Chair in Leadership at the University of Missouri-Kansas City. He has consulted to corporations, public agencies, universities, and public schools all over the world, though he generally prefers staying home with his family or meandering on mountain trails.

Lee lives in Kansas City, Missouri, with his wife, Joan Gallos. He is the coauthor with Terence Deal of numerous books, including *Escape from Cluelessness: A Guide for the Organizationally Challenged* (2000), and *The Wizard and the Warrior: Leading with Passion and Power* (2006).

Terrence E. Deal is an author, teacher, and consultant. His fascination with the symbolic side of modern organizations led to the coauthoring of the best-selling *Corporate Cultures* (1983, with A. A. Kennedy). His most recent publications include *Corporate Celebrations* and *The New Corporate Cultures*. His explorations of the world of spirit evolved from his earlier interest in the role symbols play in contemporary organizations. Terry holds a B.A. degree in history from the University of La Verne, an M.A. degree in educational administration from California State University at Los Angeles, and a Ph.D. degree in education and sociology from Stanford University. He ended his academic career as the Irving R. Melbo Professor of Education at the Rossier School, University of Southern California. He consults to business, health care, military, educational, and religious organizations both inside and outside the United States.

He lives amid vineyards and cattle on a hillside in San Luis Obispo, California, with his wife, Sandy, and their cat, Max. He is the coauthor with Lee Bolman of such books as *Reframing Organizations: Artistry, Choice and Leadership* (1997) and *Reframing the Path to School Leadership* (2010).

WRITE TO THE
AUTHORS

∞

In this book, we have shared a portion of what we have learned from many teachers. There is still much more to learn. We invite readers to participate with us in an ongoing dialogue to deepen all our understanding of spirituality in the workplace.

We know that there are many Steves, Marias, and Jills out there—in business, education, health care, government and nonprofits. We would welcome hearing your questions, your triumphs and tragedies, and your hopes and doubts about leadership and spirit at work and in life. If anything in this book touched you, troubled you, or opened new possibilities for you, please write to us. We are also interested in hearing about the sources and resources for soul and spirit that are meaningful for you. We'll respond and do our best to orchestrate an ongoing conversation. Through shared dialogue, we hope to keep finding new ways to breathe zest and joy into life and work.

You can contact us in two ways:

1. Via e-mail:

   Lee: lee@bolman.com

   Terry: sucha@surfnetusa.com

2. By postal mail:

   Lee Bolman and Terry Deal

   c/o Jossey-Bass Management Series

   Jossey-Bass/Wiley

   One Montgomery Street

   Suite 1200

   San Francisco, CA 94104